Discov

Days of Sunshine

An Interactive Daily

Prayer Journal

SATIN HOUSE PUBLISHING

Discovering 365 Days of Sunshine

An Interactive Daily Prayer Journal

Marionne Antoinette

Solid House Publishing, LLC

SHP www.solidhousepublishing.com
Founder and CEO: Gretchen Jones Torbert, Ph.D., CHLC

ISBN: 978-1-938329-79-1

Ordering Information:
Quantity sales. Special discounts are available on quantity purchases by corporations, associations, and others. For details, contact the publisher at the address above.

Orders by U.S. trade bookstores and wholesalers. Please contact Big Distribution:
Tel: (800) 401-3603; visit www.solidhousepublishing.com

Printed in the United States of America
Publisher's Cataloging-in-Publication data

p. cm.

First Edition
14 13 12 11 10 / 10 9 8 7 6 5 4 3 2 1

Dedication

This journal is first dedicated to God the Father, Son and Holy Spirit, who gave me the words to write and who gave me the stamina to give birth to this vision even though I felt extremely unqualified to be creating something for others to get closer to Him. "Thank you, Father, for choosing to use me."

This journal is dedicated to my parents Homer (R.I.P) & Mary for raising me up in the fear and admonition of the Lord and giving me a solid foundation in Christ. It is my mother's words I will always vividly remember telling my brother, Orential and me, "Whatever you do in life, do your very best! I don't care if you are a sanitation worker picking up trash. Be the best sanitation worker you can be!" These words have caused me to give my all to everything I do in life. "Thank you, mom and dad, for not being perfect parents, but being perfect parents for me. I love you!"

This journal is dedicated to the three loves of my life: Nevaeh (Heartbeat 1), Ayinde (Heartbeat 2) and Nkosi (Heartbeat 3). There aren't enough words I could ever utter to tell you how much joy and "Sunshine" you bring to my life every day. You have truly given me more to live for than anything or anyone else. You experience not only "Sunshine", but you see me when I'm not "Sunshine" and yet you love me with all my imperfections. "Mommy loves you all more than you'll ever know. Remember, there are no limits in life. Go forth and do the work God has for you. And as my mom told me, 'whatever you do in life, do your very best!' That's all mommy expects: your very best."

This journal is dedicated to the single parent who feels alone with raising your child(ren). God sees your tears and feels your pain and hasn't left you. Use this journal to draw nearer to the Father. The closer you draw to Him, the more you'll begin to realize you and your child(ren) aren't alone. "Stay encouraged my brother/sister. You have what it takes to raise up the child(ren) God has entrusted to you. I'm praying for you daily."

This journal is dedicated to Rev. Dr. Cynthia L. Hale for being a Spiritual Mother and cultivating my spiritual walk as a young adult into adulthood. Because of you, I am. I'm thankful for your leadership and guidance.

This journal is dedicated to YOU for deciding to make this journal a part of your daily life. I thank God for this work and pray that it blesses you and helps you to draw closer to the Father on a daily basis. Someday, when we are on the other side, it will be a joy to meet all those who were touched by this journal.

-~Marionne Antoinette~

Foreward

Fredrick Heiler says that "prayer is the daily business of the Christian." Prayer is conversation with God. It is sharing with God whatever is on our hearts, our joys and our sorrows, successes and struggles, dreams and hopes for tomorrow. We can talk to God about anything and everything. All those things that we are hesitant to share with anyone else, God already knows and loves us. So, we don't have to be ashamed to tell him whatever is on our hearts and minds.

Prayer is casting all our care upon God. All the things that challenge us as we seek to make a living and a life, when we release these things to him, we will discover that God cares about them more than you do. And, if we let him, he will work it out.

Prayer is also communion with God. It is spending time in his presence, enjoying his company, being filled to overflowing with his joy and peace.

Prayer is the privilege that we have been blessed with as sons and daughters of God. While each of us knows that we should pray daily, we often struggle to do so. We allow the business of life to deter us and cause us to miss out on one of the greatest joys of life. I love the way the songwriter affirms this when he says, "Oh, what peace we often forfeit. Oh, what needless pain we bear. All because we do not carry everything to God in prayer."

Our prayer and devotional life are a vital part of who we are. Marionne Antoinette has created this wonderful devotional guide that makes it easy and even fun to commune and have conversations with God each day of the year. She wants to make sure that we have an interactive journal of 365 Days of Sunshine in our lives so that we can live it to the fullest. Enjoy!

~Cynthia L. Hale, Senior Pastor, Ray of Hope Christian Church~

My Precious Reader,

It took me a very long time to birth this journal, a vision God gave me years ago. However, I birthed it out, even while feeling extremely un-qualified, just for YOU. I pray it blesses you, brings you closer to God and helps you on your daily spiritual walk. I want you to maximize the usage of this journal. See below how it was designed to be used.

How to Use this Journal

1.Use your Journal daily to draw near to God and His Word (Psalm 145:18-19)

2.Each month has a Scripture focus. Read and meditate on this scripture every day for that month. On the first day of the month, write your thoughts about this scripture in the space provided. By the end of the month, this scripture should be memorized and in your heart. (Psalm 119:11)

3.Read the month's Reflection and Prayer on the first day of each month. Let the theme resonate with you for the month. Feel free to reread the reflection and prayer any time of the month.

4.Every day, a scripture is provided. Look up that scripture reference and write the scripture out on the lines provided. Open up and allow God to minister, transform and speak to you through this scripture. Let the scripture guide your actions and thought process for the day.

5.Prayer is a privilege and God wants to hear from you. Every day, there is a "Talk to God" section provided. Write your prayers out to the Father. Be open, transparent and honest with God. This journal is between you and Him. Cast your cares on Him through this journal for He truly cares for you. (1 Peter 5:7)

6.Often times, we overlook the things God is doing in our lives daily. I want you to be intentional and look for the "Sunshine" every day and write it in your journal in the "What Sunshine did you experience for today" section.

(God prevented you from having an accident, you were late to work, but you got there safely, you didn't run out of gas, someone treated you to lunch, you received an unexpected check, your doctor's report came back in your favor, etc). Be intentional about looking for the "Sunshine" in each day and tell God "Thank You."

As you begin to write your "Sunshine" out, you will be able to go back and see God's work at hand.

We serve an awesome and amazing God who desires to commune with us daily. Allow this journal to help you do so.

His Willing Vessel,

Marionne Antoinette

Sunshine Loves You!

January's
Scripture Focus

Eye has not seen, nor ear heard,

Nor have entered into the heart of man

the things which God has prepared

for those who love Him.

I Corinthians 2:9 NKJV

My thoughts about this Scripture:

_____

_____

_____

_____

_____

_____

God loves you MORE!

Sunshine Loves You!

January's
Reflection & Prayer

This is a GREAT MONTH to start anew and bid farewell to last year. Focus no more on your losses, your downfalls or what you thought was going to happen last year. Welcome this new year and this new month with all of the opportunities it will present you. Be open to God doing something new and extraordinary in your life. Remember, God has a way of sending us opportunities that may not look like what we thought they would look like. Listen closely for and to God's voice to see and hear the new possibilities he has awaiting just for you.

Father, I thank you for this new month and this new year. May my eyes be open to receive the new opportunities you have in store for me. Release all of my fear and anxiety that comes along with doing anything new. Help me to listen closely for your voice and to move when you say move. Remove distractions from my life that would cause me to stray from you or to doubt what you are doing in my life. Thank you in advance for both my new opportunities that will expand my territory and for my new challenges that will make me stronger.

In Jesus' Name,
AMEN.

God loves you MORE!

January 2021 (United States)

February 2021

S	M	T	W	T	F	S
	1	2	3	4	5	6
7	8	9	10	11	12	13
14	15	16	17	18	19	20
21	22	23	24	25	26	27
28						

Sun	Mon	Tue	Wed	Thu	Fri	Sat
27	28	29	30	31 New Year's Eve	1 ● New Year's Day	2
3	4	5	6	7	8	9
10	11	12	13	14	15	16
17	18 ● Martin Luther King Jr. Day	19	20	21	22	23
24	25	26	27	28	29	30
31	1	2	3	4	5	6

● Federal Holidays   ● Local Holidays   ●● Multiple Events

Sunshine Loves You!

January 1, 2021

Write It Out & Meditate...

Isaiah 43:18-19

_____
_____
_____
_____
_____

Talk to God...

_____
_____
_____
_____
_____
_____
_____
_____
_____
_____

God loves you MORE!

What "SUNSHINE" did you experience today?

_____

_____

_____

_____

_____

_____

_____

_____

_____

_____

_____

_____

_____

_____

_____

_____

_____

_____

_____

Sunshine Loves You!

Write It Out & Meditate...

Isaiah 41:10

_____
_____
_____
_____
_____

Talk to God...

_____
_____
_____
_____
_____
_____
_____
_____
_____
_____
_____

God loves you MORE!

What "SUNSHINE" did you experience today?

_____

_____

_____

_____

_____

_____

_____

_____

_____

_____

_____

_____

_____

_____

_____

_____

_____

Sunshine Loves You!

January 3, 2021

Write It Out & Meditate...

Philippians 4:19

_____

_____

_____

_____

_____

Talk to God...

_____

_____

_____

_____

_____

_____

_____

_____

_____

_____

_____

God loves you MORE!

What "SUNSHINE" did you experience today?

_____

_____

_____

_____

_____

_____

_____

_____

_____

_____

_____

_____

_____

_____

_____

_____

_____

_____

_____

_____

Sunshine Loves You!

January 4, 2021

Write It Out & Meditate...

Jeremiah 33:3

_____
_____
_____
_____
_____

Talk to God...

_____
_____
_____
_____
_____
_____
_____
_____
_____
_____
_____

God loves you MORE!

What "SUNSHINE" did you experience today?

_____

_____

_____

_____

_____

_____

_____

_____

_____

_____

_____

_____

_____

_____

_____

_____

_____

_____

_____

_____

Sunshine Loves You!

January 5, 2021

Write It Out & Meditate...

Isaiah 26:3

_____
_____
_____
_____
_____

Talk to God...

_____
_____
_____
_____
_____
_____
_____
_____
_____
_____

God loves you MORE!

What "SUNSHINE" did you experience today?

_____

_____

_____

_____

_____

_____

_____

_____

_____

_____

_____

_____

_____

_____

_____

_____

_____

Sunshine Loves You!

Write It Out & Meditate...

Psalm 23:1

_____
_____
_____
_____
_____

Talk to God...

_____
_____
_____
_____
_____
_____
_____
_____
_____
_____
_____

God loves you MORE!

What "SUNSHINE" did you experience today?

_____

_____

_____

_____

_____

_____

_____

_____

_____

_____

_____

_____

_____

_____

_____

_____

_____

_____

Sunshine Loves You!

Write It Out & Meditate...

Daniel 9:9

_____
_____
_____
_____
_____

Talk to God...

_____
_____
_____
_____
_____
_____
_____
_____
_____
_____
_____

God loves you MORE!

What "SUNSHINE" did you experience today?

_____

_____

_____

_____

_____

_____

_____

_____

_____

_____

_____

_____

_____

_____

_____

_____

_____

_____

Sunshine Loves You!

Write It Out & Meditate...

2nd Corinthians 5:17

_____

_____

_____

_____

_____

Talk to God...

_____

_____

_____

_____

_____

_____

_____

_____

_____

_____

_____

God loves you MORE!

What "SUNSHINE" did you experience today?

_____

_____

_____

_____

_____

_____

_____

_____

_____

_____

_____

_____

_____

_____

_____

_____

_____

_____

Sunshine Loves You!

January 9, 2021

Write It Out & Meditate...

Genesis 28:15

_____
_____
_____
_____
_____

Talk to God...

_____
_____
_____
_____
_____
_____
_____
_____
_____
_____
_____

God loves you MORE!

What "SUNSHINE" did you experience today?

_____

_____

_____

_____

_____

_____

_____

_____

_____

_____

_____

_____

_____

_____

_____

_____

_____

_____

Sunshine Loves You!

Write It Out & Meditate...

Ezekiel 36:26

_____
_____
_____
_____
_____

Talk to God...

_____
_____
_____
_____
_____
_____
_____
_____
_____
_____
_____

God loves you MORE!

What "SUNSHINE" did you experience today?

_____

_____

_____

_____

_____

_____

_____

_____

_____

_____

_____

_____

_____

_____

_____

_____

_____

_____

_____

Sunshine Loves You!

January 11, 2021

Write It Out & Meditate...

Habakkuk 3:19

_____
_____
_____
_____
_____

Talk to God...

_____
_____
_____
_____
_____
_____
_____
_____
_____
_____
_____

God loves you MORE!

What "SUNSHINE" did you experience today?

_____

_____

_____

_____

_____

_____

_____

_____

_____

_____

_____

_____

_____

_____

_____

_____

_____

_____

_____

Sunshine Loves You!

Write It Out & Meditate...

John 16:33

_____
_____
_____
_____
_____

Talk to God...

_____
_____
_____
_____
_____
_____
_____
_____
_____
_____

God loves you MORE!

What "SUNSHINE" did you experience today?

_____

_____

_____

_____

_____

_____

_____

_____

_____

_____

_____

_____

_____

_____

_____

_____

_____

_____

Sunshine Loves You!

January 13, 2021

Write It Out & Meditate...

2nd Peter 1:3

_____

_____

_____

_____

_____

Talk to God...

_____

_____

_____

_____

_____

_____

_____

_____

_____

_____

_____

God loves you MORE!

What "SUNSHINE" did you experience today?

_____

_____

_____

_____

_____

_____

_____

_____

_____

_____

_____

_____

_____

_____

_____

_____

_____

_____

Sunshine Loves You!

Write It Out & Meditate...

Isaiah 58:11

_____
_____
_____
_____
_____

Talk to God...

_____
_____
_____
_____
_____
_____
_____
_____
_____
_____
_____

God loves you MORE!

What "SUNSHINE" did you experience today?

_____

_____

_____

_____

_____

_____

_____

_____

_____

_____

_____

_____

_____

_____

_____

_____

_____

_____

_____

_____

Sunshine Loves You!

Write It Out & Meditate...

Jeremiah 31:13

_____

_____

_____

_____

_____

Talk to God...

_____

_____

_____

_____

_____

_____

_____

_____

_____

_____

God loves you MORE!

What "SUNSHINE" did you experience today?

_____

_____

_____

_____

_____

_____

_____

_____

_____

_____

_____

_____

_____

_____

_____

_____

_____

_____

_____

_____

Sunshine Loves You!

Write It Out & Meditate...

Acts 1:11

_____

_____

_____

_____

_____

Talk to God...

_____

_____

_____

_____

_____

_____

_____

_____

_____

_____

God loves you MORE!

What "SUNSHINE" did you experience today?

_____

_____

_____

_____

_____

_____

_____

_____

_____

_____

_____

_____

_____

_____

_____

_____

_____

_____

_____

Sunshine Loves You!

Write It Out & Meditate...

Deuteronomy 20:4

_____
_____
_____
_____
_____

Talk to God...

_____
_____
_____
_____
_____
_____
_____
_____
_____
_____
_____

God loves you MORE!

What "SUNSHINE" did you experience today?

_____

_____

_____

_____

_____

_____

_____

_____

_____

_____

_____

_____

_____

_____

_____

_____

_____

_____

_____

Sunshine Loves You!

Write It Out & Meditate...

Psalm 32:8

_____

_____

_____

_____

_____

Talk to God...

_____

_____

_____

_____

_____

_____

_____

_____

_____

_____

_____

God loves you MORE!

What "SUNSHINE" did you experience today?

_____

_____

_____

_____

_____

_____

_____

_____

_____

_____

_____

_____

_____

_____

_____

_____

_____

_____

Sunshine Loves You!

Write It Out & Meditate...

Galatians 3:29

_____

_____

_____

_____

_____

Talk to God...

_____

_____

_____

_____

_____

_____

_____

_____

_____

_____

God loves you MORE!

What "SUNSHINE" did you experience today?

_____

_____

_____

_____

_____

_____

_____

_____

_____

_____

_____

_____

_____

_____

_____

_____

_____

_____

_____

_____

Sunshine Loves You!

January 20, 2021

Write It Out & Meditate...

Genesis 12:3

_____
_____
_____
_____
_____

Talk to God...

_____
_____
_____
_____
_____
_____
_____
_____
_____
_____
_____

God loves you MORE!

What "SUNSHINE" did you experience today?

_____

_____

_____

_____

_____

_____

_____

_____

_____

_____

_____

_____

_____

_____

_____

_____

_____

_____

_____

_____

Sunshine Loves You!

January 21, 2021

Write It Out & Meditate...

2nd Timothy 1:7

_____
_____
_____
_____
_____

Talk to God...

_____
_____
_____
_____
_____
_____
_____
_____
_____
_____
_____

God loves you MORE!

What "SUNSHINE" did you experience today?

_____

_____

_____

_____

_____

_____

_____

_____

_____

_____

_____

_____

_____

_____

_____

_____

_____

_____

_____

Sunshine Loves You!

Write It Out & Meditate...

Hebrews 10:36

_____

_____

_____

_____

_____

Talk to God...

_____

_____

_____

_____

_____

_____

_____

_____

_____

_____

God loves you MORE!

What "SUNSHINE" did you experience today?

_____

_____

_____

_____

_____

_____

_____

_____

_____

_____

_____

_____

_____

_____

_____

_____

_____

_____

_____

_____

Sunshine Loves You!

Write It Out & Meditate...

Psalm 37:23-24

_____

_____

_____

_____

_____

Talk to God...

_____

_____

_____

_____

_____

_____

_____

_____

_____

_____

_____

God loves you MORE!

What "SUNSHINE" did you experience today?

_____

_____

_____

_____

_____

_____

_____

_____

_____

_____

_____

_____

_____

_____

_____

_____

_____

_____

Sunshine Loves You!

January 24, 2021

Write It Out & Meditate...

Matthew 11:28-30

_____
_____
_____
_____
_____

Talk to God...

_____
_____
_____
_____
_____
_____
_____
_____
_____
_____

God loves you MORE!

What "SUNSHINE" did you experience today?

_____

_____

_____

_____

_____

_____

_____

_____

_____

_____

_____

_____

_____

_____

_____

_____

_____

_____

Sunshine Loves You!

Write It Out & Meditate...

1st John 1:9

_____
_____
_____
_____
_____

Talk to God...

_____
_____
_____
_____
_____
_____
_____
_____
_____
_____

God loves you MORE!

What "SUNSHINE" did you experience today?

_____

_____

_____

_____

_____

_____

_____

_____

_____

_____

_____

_____

_____

_____

_____

_____

_____

_____

Sunshine Loves You!

Write It Out & Meditate...

2nd Cornithians 12:9-10

_____

_____

_____

_____

_____

Talk to God...

_____

_____

_____

_____

_____

_____

_____

_____

_____

_____

_____

_____

God loves you MORE!

What "SUNSHINE" did you experience today?

_____

_____

_____

_____

_____

_____

_____

_____

_____

_____

_____

_____

_____

_____

_____

_____

_____

Sunshine Loves You!

Write It Out & Meditate...

Isaiah 12:2

_____

_____

_____

_____

_____

Talk to God...

_____

_____

_____

_____

_____

_____

_____

_____

_____

_____

_____

God loves you MORE!

What "SUNSHINE" did you experience today?

_____

_____

_____

_____

_____

_____

_____

_____

_____

_____

_____

_____

_____

_____

_____

_____

_____

_____

Sunshine Loves You!

Write It Out & Meditate...

Jeremiah 15:21

_____

_____

_____

_____

_____

Talk to God...

_____

_____

_____

_____

_____

_____

_____

_____

_____

_____

_____

God loves you MORE!

What "SUNSHINE" did you experience today?

_____

_____

_____

_____

_____

_____

_____

_____

_____

_____

_____

_____

_____

_____

_____

_____

_____

_____

_____

Sunshine Loves You!

Write It Out & Meditate...

Matthew 6:3-4

_____

_____

_____

_____

_____

Talk to God...

_____

_____

_____

_____

_____

_____

_____

_____

_____

_____

God loves you MORE!

What "SUNSHINE" did you experience today?

_____

_____

_____

_____

_____

_____

_____

_____

_____

_____

_____

_____

_____

_____

_____

_____

_____

Sunshine Loves You!

Write It Out & Meditate...

Psalm 23:4

_____

_____

_____

_____

_____

Talk to God...

_____

_____

_____

_____

_____

_____

_____

_____

_____

_____

_____

God loves you MORE!

What "SUNSHINE" did you experience today?

_____

_____

_____

_____

_____

_____

_____

_____

_____

_____

_____

_____

_____

_____

_____

_____

_____

_____

Sunshine Loves You!

Write It Out & Meditate...

Isaiah 40:31

_____
_____
_____
_____
_____

Talk to God...

_____
_____
_____
_____
_____
_____
_____
_____
_____
_____

God loves you MORE!

What "SUNSHINE" did you experience today?

_____

_____

_____

_____

_____

_____

_____

_____

_____

_____

_____

_____

_____

_____

_____

_____

_____

Sunshine Loves You!

February's
Scripture Focus

We love because he first loved us.

1 John 4:19 NIV

My thoughts about this Scripture:

_____

_____

_____

_____

_____

_____

_____

_____

_____

_____

God loves you MORE!

Sunshine Loves You!

February's
Reflection & Prayer

This is a GREAT MONTH to make amends with someone who has been unkind or unfriendly and far from Godly. Be the bigger individual and do your part to make amends (even if you weren't wrong). Look deeply to see the good in this individual, as you begin to discover a bit of God in them. Often times, being "mean" is a cry for help. You are the right person to help this individual. Experience God's presence as you forgive those who have wronged you. Remember, God loves us even when we turn our back on Him. Remember, God loves us even when we do things out of His will. Remember, God loves us even when we intentionally disobey Him. His love is unchanging. Let's begin to ask God to put an unchanging love in us towards others so that we may begin to look more like Him.

Father, I thank you that your love for me has never changed even when I was ever changing. Thank you for allowing me to experience true love from You. Help me to build up a love for others that would allow me to see past their faults; yet, to see their need to be loved. Let your love resonate in and around me so that I may spread the love of Christ to others who are in search of you.

In Jesus' Name,
AMEN.

God loves you MORE!

February 2021 (United States)

March 2021

S	M	T	W	T	F	S
	1	2	3	4	5	6
7	8	9	10	11	12	13
14	15	16	17	18	19	20
21	22	23	24	25	26	27
28	29	30	31			

Sun	Mon	Tue	Wed	Thu	Fri	Sat
31	1 First Day of Black History Month	2	3	4 ☽ 3rd Quarter	5	6
7	8	9	10	11 ● New Moon	12	13
14 Valentine's Day	15 ● Presidents' Day (Most regions)	16	17	18	19 ☾ 1st Quarter	20
21	22	23	24	25	26	27 ○ Full Moon
28	1 First Day of Black History Month	2	3	4	5 ☽ 3rd Quarter	6

Sunshine Loves You!

Write It Out & Meditate...

Philippians 4:6-7

_____
_____
_____
_____
_____

Talk to God...

_____
_____
_____
_____
_____
_____
_____
_____
_____

God loves you MORE!

What "SUNSHINE" did you experience today?

_____

_____

_____

_____

_____

_____

_____

_____

_____

_____

_____

_____

_____

_____

_____

_____

_____

_____

_____

_____

Sunshine Loves You!

Write It Out & Meditate...

1st Peter 2:24

_____
_____
_____
_____
_____

Talk to God...

_____
_____
_____
_____
_____
_____
_____
_____
_____
_____
_____

God loves you MORE!

What "SUNSHINE" did you experience today?

_____

_____

_____

_____

_____

_____

_____

_____

_____

_____

_____

_____

_____

_____

_____

_____

_____

_____

_____

_____

_____

Sunshine Loves You!

Write It Out & Meditate...

James 1:2-3

_____

_____

_____

_____

_____

Talk to God...

_____

_____

_____

_____

_____

_____

_____

_____

_____

_____

_____

God loves you MORE!

What "SUNSHINE" did you experience today?

_____

_____

_____

_____

_____

_____

_____

_____

_____

_____

_____

_____

_____

_____

_____

_____

_____

_____

_____

Sunshine Loves You!

Write It Out & Meditate...

Matthew 18:19

_____

_____

_____

_____

_____

Talk to God...

_____

_____

_____

_____

_____

_____

_____

_____

_____

_____

_____

God loves you MORE!

What "SUNSHINE" did you experience today?

_____

_____

_____

_____

_____

_____

_____

_____

_____

_____

_____

_____

_____

_____

_____

_____

_____

_____

Sunshine Loves You!

February 5, 2021

Write It Out & Meditate...

Proverbs 16:3

_____
_____
_____
_____
_____

Talk to God...

_____
_____
_____
_____
_____
_____
_____
_____
_____
_____

God loves you MORE!

What "SUNSHINE" did you experience today?

_____

_____

_____

_____

_____

_____

_____

_____

_____

_____

_____

_____

_____

_____

_____

_____

_____

Sunshine Loves You!

Write It Out & Meditate...

Deuteronomy 8:5

_____

_____

_____

_____

_____

Talk to God...

_____

_____

_____

_____

_____

_____

_____

_____

_____

_____

_____

God loves you MORE!

What "SUNSHINE" did you experience today?

_____

_____

_____

_____

_____

_____

_____

_____

_____

_____

_____

_____

_____

_____

_____

_____

_____

_____

Sunshine Loves You!

February 7, 2021

Write It Out & Meditate...

Colossians 3:23-24

_____
_____
_____
_____
_____

Talk to God...

_____
_____
_____
_____
_____
_____
_____
_____
_____
_____
_____

God loves you MORE!

What "SUNSHINE" did you experience today?

_____

_____

_____

_____

_____

_____

_____

_____

_____

_____

_____

_____

_____

_____

_____

_____

_____

Sunshine Loves You!

Write It Out & Meditate...

John 6:40

_____

_____

_____

_____

_____

Talk to God...

_____

_____

_____

_____

_____

_____

_____

_____

_____

_____

_____

God loves you MORE!

What "SUNSHINE" did you experience today?

_____

_____

_____

_____

_____

_____

_____

_____

_____

_____

_____

_____

_____

_____

_____

_____

_____

_____

Sunshine Loves You!

February 9, 2021

Write It Out & Meditate...

Exodus 14:14

_____
_____
_____
_____
_____

Talk to God...

_____
_____
_____
_____
_____
_____
_____
_____
_____
_____

God loves you MORE!

What "SUNSHINE" did you experience today?

_____

_____

_____

_____

_____

_____

_____

_____

_____

_____

_____

_____

_____

_____

_____

_____

_____

Sunshine Loves You!

Write It Out & Meditate...

Psalm 91:3

_____

_____

_____

_____

_____

Talk to God...

_____

_____

_____

_____

_____

_____

_____

_____

_____

_____

God loves you MORE!

What "SUNSHINE" did you experience today?

_____

_____

_____

_____

_____

_____

_____

_____

_____

_____

_____

_____

_____

_____

_____

_____

_____

Sunshine Loves You!

Write It Out & Meditate...

Psalm 32:5

_____

_____

_____

_____

_____

Talk to God...

_____

_____

_____

_____

_____

_____

_____

_____

_____

_____

God loves you MORE!

What "SUNSHINE" did you experience today?

_____

_____

_____

_____

_____

_____

_____

_____

_____

_____

_____

_____

_____

_____

_____

_____

Sunshine Loves You!

February 12, 2021

Write It Out & Meditate...

Exodus 20:12

_____

_____

_____

_____

_____

Talk to God...

_____

_____

_____

_____

_____

_____

_____

_____

_____

_____

_____

God loves you MORE!

What "SUNSHINE" did you experience today?

_____

_____

_____

_____

_____

_____

_____

_____

_____

_____

_____

_____

_____

_____

_____

_____

_____

_____

_____

Sunshine Loves You!

Write It Out & Meditate...

1st Corinthians 10:13

_____
_____
_____
_____
_____

Talk to God...

_____
_____
_____
_____
_____
_____
_____
_____
_____
_____
_____

God loves you MORE!

What "SUNSHINE" did you experience today?

_____

_____

_____

_____

_____

_____

_____

_____

_____

_____

_____

_____

_____

_____

_____

_____

_____

_____

Sunshine Loves You!

Write It Out & Meditate...

John 15:13

_____
_____
_____
_____
_____

Talk to God...

_____
_____
_____
_____
_____
_____
_____
_____
_____
_____
_____

God loves you MORE!

What "SUNSHINE" did you experience today?

_____

_____

_____

_____

_____

_____

_____

_____

_____

_____

_____

_____

_____

_____

_____

_____

_____

_____

_____

Sunshine Loves You!

February 15, 2021

Write It Out & Meditate...

Zephaniah 3:17

_____
_____
_____
_____
_____

Talk to God...

_____
_____
_____
_____
_____
_____
_____
_____
_____
_____
_____

God loves you MORE!

What "SUNSHINE" did you experience today?

_____

_____

_____

_____

_____

_____

_____

_____

_____

_____

_____

_____

_____

_____

_____

_____

_____

_____

_____

_____

Sunshine Loves You!

Write It Out & Meditate...

Philippians 4:8

_____

_____

_____

_____

_____

Talk to God...

_____

_____

_____

_____

_____

_____

_____

_____

_____

_____

God loves you MORE!

What "SUNSHINE" did you experience today?

_____

_____

_____

_____

_____

_____

_____

_____

_____

_____

_____

_____

_____

_____

_____

_____

_____

_____

Sunshine Loves You!

Write It Out & Meditate...

Isaiah 40:29

_____

_____

_____

_____

_____

Talk to God...

_____

_____

_____

_____

_____

_____

_____

_____

_____

_____

God loves you MORE!

What "SUNSHINE" did you experience today?

_____

_____

_____

_____

_____

_____

_____

_____

_____

_____

_____

_____

_____

_____

_____

_____

_____

_____

Sunshine Loves You!

February 18, 2021

Write It Out & Meditate...

Zechariah 13:9

_____
_____
_____
_____
_____

Talk to God...

_____
_____
_____
_____
_____
_____
_____
_____
_____
_____

God loves you MORE!

What "SUNSHINE" did you experience today?

_____

_____

_____

_____

_____

_____

_____

_____

_____

_____

_____

_____

_____

_____

_____

_____

_____

_____

Sunshine Loves You!

Write It Out & Meditate...

Deuteronomy 10:21

_____

_____

_____

_____

_____

Talk to God...

_____

_____

_____

_____

_____

_____

_____

_____

_____

_____

God loves you MORE!

What "SUNSHINE" did you experience today?

_____

_____

_____

_____

_____

_____

_____

_____

_____

_____

_____

_____

_____

_____

_____

_____

_____

_____

Sunshine Loves You!

Write It Out & Meditate...

Numbers 14:8

_____

_____

_____

_____

_____

Talk to God...

_____

_____

_____

_____

_____

_____

_____

_____

_____

_____

_____

God loves you MORE!

What "SUNSHINE" did you experience today?

_____

_____

_____

_____

_____

_____

_____

_____

_____

_____

_____

_____

_____

_____

_____

_____

_____

_____

Sunshine Loves You!

Write It Out & Meditate...

1st Thessalonians 4:3

_____

_____

_____

_____

_____

Talk to God...

_____

_____

_____

_____

_____

_____

_____

_____

_____

_____

_____

God loves you MORE!

What "SUNSHINE" did you experience today?

_____

_____

_____

_____

_____

_____

_____

_____

_____

_____

_____

_____

_____

_____

_____

_____

_____

Sunshine Loves You!

Write It Out & Meditate...

Isaiah 1:18

_____

_____

_____

_____

_____

Talk to God...

_____

_____

_____

_____

_____

_____

_____

_____

_____

_____

God loves you MORE!

What "SUNSHINE" did you experience today?

_____

_____

_____

_____

_____

_____

_____

_____

_____

_____

_____

_____

_____

_____

_____

_____

_____

_____

Sunshine Loves You!

Write It Out & Meditate...

2nd Samuel 14:14

_____

_____

_____

_____

_____

Talk to God...

_____

_____

_____

_____

_____

_____

_____

_____

_____

_____

God loves you MORE!

What "SUNSHINE" did you experience today?

_____

_____

_____

_____

_____

_____

_____

_____

_____

_____

_____

_____

_____

_____

_____

_____

_____

_____

Sunshine Loves You!

Write It Out & Meditate...

Isaiah 43:2

_____

_____

_____

_____

_____

Talk to God...

_____

_____

_____

_____

_____

_____

_____

_____

_____

_____

_____

God loves you MORE!

What "SUNSHINE" did you experience today?

_____

_____

_____

_____

_____

_____

_____

_____

_____

_____

_____

_____

_____

_____

_____

_____

_____

_____

Sunshine Loves You!

Write It Out & Meditate...

Matthew 7:8

_____

_____

_____

_____

_____

Talk to God...

_____

_____

_____

_____

_____

_____

_____

_____

_____

_____

_____

_____

God loves you MORE!

What "SUNSHINE" did you experience today?

_____

_____

_____

_____

_____

_____

_____

_____

_____

_____

_____

_____

_____

_____

_____

_____

_____

Sunshine Loves You!

Write It Out & Meditate...

Psalm 68:19

_____

_____

_____

_____

_____

Talk to God...

_____

_____

_____

_____

_____

_____

_____

_____

_____

_____

_____

God loves you MORE!

What "SUNSHINE" did you experience today?

_____

_____

_____

_____

_____

_____

_____

_____

_____

_____

_____

_____

_____

_____

_____

_____

_____

_____

Sunshine Loves You!

Write It Out & Meditate...

Isaiah 54:10

_____

_____

_____

_____

_____

Talk to God...

_____

_____

_____

_____

_____

_____

_____

_____

_____

_____

God loves you MORE!

What "SUNSHINE" did you experience today?

_____

_____

_____

_____

_____

_____

_____

_____

_____

_____

_____

_____

_____

_____

_____

_____

_____

_____

_____

Sunshine Loves You!

Write It Out & Meditate...

1st Peter 2:9

_____

_____

_____

_____

_____

Talk to God...

_____

_____

_____

_____

_____

_____

_____

_____

_____

_____

_____

God loves you MORE!

What "SUNSHINE" did you experience today?

_____

_____

_____

_____

_____

_____

_____

_____

_____

_____

_____

_____

_____

_____

_____

_____

_____

_____

Sunshine Loves You!

March's

Scripture Focus

He answered their prayers,

because they trusted in him.

1 Chronicles 5:20 NIV

My thoughts about this Scripture:

_____

_____

_____

_____

_____

_____

_____

_____

God loves you MORE!

Sunshine Loves You!

March's
Reflection & Prayer

This is a GREAT MONTH to confide in God. Start talking more to God and less to people. God listens to you without judgment. Tell God your Faith is childlike and your trust in Him has matured. Stop operating in your own strength. Put your battles before God in prayer this month and claim your victories in advance. Every problem has a solution. Ask God to reveal the solution to you and make you a part of the solution.

Father, I thank you that you hear my prayers. Please forgive me for trying to handle my battles and situations on my own. I now realize I need to trust you more because you are the Creator and you know all and see all. I know you are a BIG GOD and specialize in fighting battles and handling situations I am unable to handle. I trust you and I give every battle over to you to fight for me this day forward. I put my hands down to trying to handle situations in my own strength and put my hands up in submission and surrender all to You. I trust you God. Thank you in advance for the many victories I will see simply because I trust you.

In Jesus' Name,
AMEN.

God loves you MORE!

March 2021 (United States)

April 2021
S M T W T F S
1 2 3
4 5 6 7 8 9 10
11 12 13 14 15 16 17
18 19 20 21 22 23 24
25 26 27 28 29 30

Sun	Mon	Tue	Wed	Thu	Fri	Sat
28	1	2	3	4	5	6
7	8	9	10	11	12	13
14	15	16	17 St. Patrick's Day	18	19	20
21	22	23	24	25	26	27
28	29	30	31	1	2	3

● Federal Holidays   ● Local Holidays   ●● Religion Events

Sunshine Loves You!

Write It Out & Meditate...

Acts 16:31

_____

_____

_____

_____

_____

Talk to God...

_____

_____

_____

_____

_____

_____

_____

_____

_____

_____

God loves you MORE!

What "SUNSHINE" did you experience today?

_____

_____

_____

_____

_____

_____

_____

_____

_____

_____

_____

_____

_____

_____

_____

_____

_____

_____

_____

Sunshine Loves You!

Write It Out & Meditate...

Deuteronomy 31:6

_____

_____

_____

_____

_____

Talk to God...

_____

_____

_____

_____

_____

_____

_____

_____

_____

_____

God loves you MORE!

What "SUNSHINE" did you experience today?

_____

_____

_____

_____

_____

_____

_____

_____

_____

_____

_____

_____

_____

_____

_____

_____

_____

Sunshine Loves You!

March 3, 2021

Write It Out & Meditate...

Ephesians 1:7

_____

_____

_____

_____

_____

Talk to God...

_____

_____

_____

_____

_____

_____

_____

_____

_____

_____

_____

God loves you MORE!

What "SUNSHINE" did you experience today?

_____

_____

_____

_____

_____

_____

_____

_____

_____

_____

_____

_____

_____

_____

_____

_____

_____

Sunshine Loves You!

March 4, 2021

Write It Out & Meditate...

_____

_____

_____

_____

_____

Talk to God...

_____

_____

_____

_____

_____

_____

_____

_____

_____

_____

God loves you MORE!

What "SUNSHINE" did you experience today?

_____

_____

_____

_____

_____

_____

_____

_____

_____

_____

_____

_____

_____

_____

_____

_____

_____

_____

Sunshine Loves You!

Write It Out & Meditate...

Isaiah 54:17

_____
_____
_____
_____
_____

Talk to God...

_____
_____
_____
_____
_____
_____
_____
_____
_____
_____
_____

God loves you MORE!

What "SUNSHINE" did you experience today?

_____

_____

_____

_____

_____

_____

_____

_____

_____

_____

_____

_____

_____

_____

_____

_____

_____

_____

Sunshine Loves You!

Write It Out & Meditate...

Malachi 3:6

_____
_____
_____
_____
_____

Talk to God...

_____
_____
_____
_____
_____
_____
_____
_____
_____
_____

God loves you MORE!

What "SUNSHINE" did you experience today?

_____

_____

_____

_____

_____

_____

_____

_____

_____

_____

_____

_____

_____

_____

_____

_____

_____

Sunshine Loves You!

Write It Out & Meditate...

Psalm 55:16-17

_____

_____

_____

_____

_____

Talk to God...

_____

_____

_____

_____

_____

_____

_____

_____

_____

_____

_____

God loves you MORE!

What "SUNSHINE" did you experience today?

_____

_____

_____

_____

_____

_____

_____

_____

_____

_____

_____

_____

_____

_____

_____

_____

_____

_____

_____

Sunshine Loves You!

March 8, 2021

Write It Out & Meditate...

Romans 16:20

_____

_____

_____

_____

_____

Talk to God...

_____

_____

_____

_____

_____

_____

_____

_____

_____

_____

God loves you MORE!

What "SUNSHINE" did you experience today?

_____

_____

_____

_____

_____

_____

_____

_____

_____

_____

_____

_____

_____

_____

_____

_____

_____

_____

Sunshine Loves You!

Write It Out & Meditate...

Proverbs 16:9

_____

_____

_____

_____

_____

Talk to God...

_____

_____

_____

_____

_____

_____

_____

_____

_____

_____

God loves you MORE!

What "SUNSHINE" did you experience today?

_____

_____

_____

_____

_____

_____

_____

_____

_____

_____

_____

_____

_____

_____

_____

_____

_____

_____

_____

Sunshine Loves You!

Write It Out & Meditate...

Psalm 126:5

_____

_____

_____

_____

_____

Talk to God...

_____

_____

_____

_____

_____

_____

_____

_____

_____

_____

_____

_____

God loves you MORE!

What "SUNSHINE" did you experience today?

_____

_____

_____

_____

_____

_____

_____

_____

_____

_____

_____

_____

_____

_____

_____

_____

_____

_____

_____

_____

Sunshine Loves You!

Write It Out & Meditate...

Luke 21:15

_____

_____

_____

_____

_____

Talk to God...

_____

_____

_____

_____

_____

_____

_____

_____

_____

_____

_____

God loves you MORE!

What "SUNSHINE" did you experience today?

_____

_____

_____

_____

_____

_____

_____

_____

_____

_____

_____

_____

_____

_____

_____

_____

_____

_____

_____

Sunshine Loves You!

Write It Out & Meditate...

Matthew 5:9

_____

_____

_____

_____

_____

Talk to God...

_____

_____

_____

_____

_____

_____

_____

_____

_____

_____

God loves you MORE!

What "SUNSHINE" did you experience today?

_____

_____

_____

_____

_____

_____

_____

_____

_____

_____

_____

_____

_____

_____

_____

_____

_____

_____

_____

_____

Sunshine Loves You!

Write It Out & Meditate...

James 1:17

_____

_____

_____

_____

_____

Talk to God...

_____

_____

_____

_____

_____

_____

_____

_____

_____

_____

_____

God loves you MORE!

What "SUNSHINE" did you experience today?

_____

_____

_____

_____

_____

_____

_____

_____

_____

_____

_____

_____

_____

_____

_____

_____

_____

_____

Sunshine Loves You!

Write It Out & Meditate...

John 15:17

_____

_____

_____

_____

_____

Talk to God...

_____

_____

_____

_____

_____

_____

_____

_____

_____

_____

_____

God loves you MORE!

What "SUNSHINE" did you experience today?

_____
_____
_____
_____
_____
_____
_____
_____
_____
_____
_____
_____
_____
_____
_____
_____
_____
_____
_____
_____

Sunshine Loves You!

Write It Out & Meditate...

Isaiah 61:1-2

_____

_____

_____

_____

_____

Talk to God...

_____

_____

_____

_____

_____

_____

_____

_____

_____

_____

God loves you MORE!

What "SUNSHINE" did you experience today?

_____

_____

_____

_____

_____

_____

_____

_____

_____

_____

_____

_____

_____

_____

_____

_____

_____

_____

_____

Sunshine Loves You!

Write It Out & Meditate...

Psalm 85:2

_____
_____
_____
_____
_____

Talk to God...

_____
_____
_____
_____
_____
_____
_____
_____
_____
_____
_____

God loves you MORE!

What "SUNSHINE" did you experience today?

_____

_____

_____

_____

_____

_____

_____

_____

_____

_____

_____

_____

_____

_____

_____

_____

_____

_____

_____

Sunshine Loves You!

Write It Out & Meditate...

Isaiah 41:13

_____

_____

_____

_____

_____

Talk to God...

_____

_____

_____

_____

_____

_____

_____

_____

_____

_____

_____

God loves you MORE!

What "SUNSHINE" did you experience today?

_____

_____

_____

_____

_____

_____

_____

_____

_____

_____

_____

_____

_____

_____

_____

_____

_____

_____

Sunshine Loves You!

Write It Out & Meditate...

1st Corinthians 3:8-9

_____

_____

_____

_____

_____

Talk to God...

_____

_____

_____

_____

_____

_____

_____

_____

_____

_____

_____

God loves you MORE!

What "SUNSHINE" did you experience today?

_____

_____

_____

_____

_____

_____

_____

_____

_____

_____

_____

_____

_____

_____

_____

_____

_____

_____

_____

Sunshine Loves You!

Write It Out & Meditate...

John 10:27-29

_____

_____

_____

_____

_____

Talk to God...

_____

_____

_____

_____

_____

_____

_____

_____

_____

_____

God loves you MORE!

What "SUNSHINE" did you experience today?

_____

_____

_____

_____

_____

_____

_____

_____

_____

_____

_____

_____

_____

_____

_____

_____

_____

_____

Sunshine Loves You!

Write It Out & Meditate...

Psalm 138:8

_____

_____

_____

_____

_____

Talk to God...

_____

_____

_____

_____

_____

_____

_____

_____

_____

_____

God loves you MORE!

What "SUNSHINE" did you experience today?

_____

_____

_____

_____

_____

_____

_____

_____

_____

_____

_____

_____

_____

_____

_____

_____

_____

_____

Sunshine Loves You!

Write It Out & Meditate...

Hebrews 13:5

_____

_____

_____

_____

_____

Talk to God...

_____

_____

_____

_____

_____

_____

_____

_____

_____

_____

God loves you MORE!

What "SUNSHINE" did you experience today?

_____

_____

_____

_____

_____

_____

_____

_____

_____

_____

_____

_____

_____

_____

_____

_____

_____

_____

_____

Sunshine Loves You!

Write It Out & Meditate...

John 5:24

_____

_____

_____

_____

_____

Talk to God...

_____

_____

_____

_____

_____

_____

_____

_____

_____

_____

_____

God loves you MORE!

What "SUNSHINE" did you experience today?

_____

_____

_____

_____

_____

_____

_____

_____

_____

_____

_____

_____

_____

_____

_____

_____

_____

_____

_____

Sunshine Loves You!

Write It Out & Meditate...

Acts 2:38

_____

_____

_____

_____

_____

Talk to God...

_____

_____

_____

_____

_____

_____

_____

_____

_____

_____

_____

God loves you MORE!

What "SUNSHINE" did you experience today?

_____

_____

_____

_____

_____

_____

_____

_____

_____

_____

_____

_____

_____

_____

_____

_____

_____

_____

_____

_____

Sunshine Loves You!

Write It Out & Meditate...

2nd Corinthians 10:4-5

_____

_____

_____

_____

_____

Talk to God...

_____

_____

_____

_____

_____

_____

_____

_____

_____

_____

_____

God loves you MORE!

What "SUNSHINE" did you experience today?

_____

_____

_____

_____

_____

_____

_____

_____

_____

_____

_____

_____

_____

_____

_____

_____

_____

_____

_____

Sunshine Loves You!

Write It Out & Meditate...

Psalm 27:10

_____

_____

_____

_____

_____

Talk to God...

_____

_____

_____

_____

_____

_____

_____

_____

_____

_____

_____

God loves you MORE!

What "SUNSHINE" did you experience today?

_____

_____

_____

_____

_____

_____

_____

_____

_____

_____

_____

_____

_____

_____

_____

_____

_____

_____

_____

Sunshine Loves You!

Write It Out & Meditate...

Matthew 5:42

_____

_____

_____

_____

_____

Talk to God...

_____

_____

_____

_____

_____

_____

_____

_____

_____

_____

God loves you MORE!

What "SUNSHINE" did you experience today?

_____

_____

_____

_____

_____

_____

_____

_____

_____

_____

_____

_____

_____

_____

_____

_____

_____

_____

_____

Sunshine Loves You!

Write It Out & Meditate...

Galatians 2:20

_____

_____

_____

_____

_____

Talk to God...

_____

_____

_____

_____

_____

_____

_____

_____

_____

_____

_____

God loves you MORE!

What "SUNSHINE" did you experience today?

_____

_____

_____

_____

_____

_____

_____

_____

_____

_____

_____

_____

_____

_____

_____

_____

_____

Sunshine Loves You!

Write It Out & Meditate...

Deuteronomy 31:8

_____

_____

_____

_____

_____

Talk to God...

_____

_____

_____

_____

_____

_____

_____

_____

_____

_____

_____

God loves you MORE!

What "SUNSHINE" did you experience today?

_____

_____

_____

_____

_____

_____

_____

_____

_____

_____

_____

_____

_____

_____

_____

_____

_____

_____

_____

_____

Sunshine Loves You!

Write It Out & Meditate...

Jeremiah 29:11

_____

_____

_____

_____

_____

Talk to God...

_____

_____

_____

_____

_____

_____

_____

_____

_____

_____

God loves you MORE!

What "SUNSHINE" did you experience today?

_____

_____

_____

_____

_____

_____

_____

_____

_____

_____

_____

_____

_____

_____

_____

_____

_____

_____

_____

_____

Sunshine Loves You!

Write It Out & Meditate...

Romans 8:17

_____

_____

_____

_____

_____

Talk to God...

_____

_____

_____

_____

_____

_____

_____

_____

_____

_____

God loves you MORE!

What "SUNSHINE" did you experience today?

_____

_____

_____

_____

_____

_____

_____

_____

_____

_____

_____

_____

_____

_____

_____

_____

_____

_____

_____

_____

Sunshine Loves You!

Write It Out & Meditate...

Hebrews 13:6

_____

_____

_____

_____

_____

Talk to God...

_____

_____

_____

_____

_____

_____

_____

_____

_____

_____

_____

God loves you MORE!

What "SUNSHINE" did you experience today?

_____

_____

_____

_____

_____

_____

_____

_____

_____

_____

_____

_____

_____

_____

_____

_____

_____

_____

_____

_____

Sunshine Loves You!

April's

Scripture Focus

Be strong and courageous. Do not be afraid or terrified because of them, for the Lord your God goes with you; he will never leave you nor forsake you.

Deuteronomy 31:6 NIV

My thoughts about this Scripture:

_____

_____

_____

_____

_____

_____

_____

_____

God loves you MORE!

Sunshine Loves You!

April's
Reflection & Prayer

This is a GREAT MONTH to display a faith that remains unshaken despite the onset of trials and tribulations that may arise this month. Every day, we face war: war in our minds, war on our jobs, war in our homes, war in the world, but God is with us through it all. There's no need to be afraid. Nothing takes God by surprise. Glance to your left, God is there. Glance to your right, God is there. Look in front of you, God is there. Look behind you, God is still there. God promises to never leave you. And one thing you can rest assure, is that God doesn't lie. You are surrounded and protected by the Almighty One. Walk about courageously this month knowing that God is encamped around you wherever you go.

Father, I thank you that you are my shield and my protector. I thank you that you are making me stronger and more courageous daily as I continue to learn and activate your Word. Thank you for being with me every moment of the day. Thank you for letting me know that though I may feel lonely at times, I am not alone because you are with me. Help me to talk to you more, knowing you are always there to listen to me. More importantly, help me to listen even more to You after you have given me my assignment. Many have forsaken me, but you are a consistent God and I know I can count on you to be there on my good, bad and ugly days without judgement. Thank you in advance for giving me the courage to do something this month I've always wanted to do but was afraid to do.

In Jesus' Name,
AMEN.

God loves you MORE!

April 2021 (United States)

May 2021

S	M	T	W	T	F	S
						1
2	3	4	5	6	7	8
9	10	11	12	13	14	15
16	17	18	19	20	21	22
23	24	25	26	27	28	29
30	31					

Sun	Mon	Tue	Wed	Thu	Fri	Sat
28 ○ Full Moon	29	30	31	1	2	3
4 ◑ 3rd Quarter Easter Sunday	5 Easter Monday	6	7	8	9	10
11 ● New Moon	12	13	14	15 Tax Day	16	17
18	19	20 ◐ 1st Quarter	21	22	23	24
25	26 ○ Full Moon	27	28	29	30	1

● Federal Holidays   ● Local Holidays   ●● Multiple Events

Sunshine Loves You!

April 1, 2021

Write It Out & Meditate...

Genesis 12:2

_____

_____

_____

_____

_____

Talk to God...

_____

_____

_____

_____

_____

_____

_____

_____

_____

_____

God loves you MORE!

What "SUNSHINE" did you experience today?

_____

_____

_____

_____

_____

_____

_____

_____

_____

_____

_____

_____

_____

_____

_____

_____

_____

_____

_____

Sunshine Loves You!

April 2, 2021

Write It Out & Meditate...

James 1:5

_____
_____
_____
_____
_____

Talk to God...

_____
_____
_____
_____
_____
_____
_____
_____
_____
_____
_____

God loves you MORE!

What "SUNSHINE" did you experience today?

_____

_____

_____

_____

_____

_____

_____

_____

_____

_____

_____

_____

_____

_____

_____

_____

_____

_____

_____

Sunshine Loves You!

Write It Out & Meditate...

Ephesians 5:8

_____
_____
_____
_____
_____

Talk to God...

_____
_____
_____
_____
_____
_____
_____
_____
_____
_____
_____

God loves you MORE!

What "SUNSHINE" did you experience today?

_____

_____

_____

_____

_____

_____

_____

_____

_____

_____

_____

_____

_____

_____

_____

_____

_____

_____

_____

_____

Sunshine Loves You!

Write It Out & Meditate...

James 4:7

_____

_____

_____

_____

_____

Talk to God...

_____

_____

_____

_____

_____

_____

_____

_____

_____

_____

God loves you MORE!

What "SUNSHINE" did you experience today?

_____

_____

_____

_____

_____

_____

_____

_____

_____

_____

_____

_____

_____

_____

_____

_____

_____

_____

_____

_____

_____

Sunshine Loves You!

April 5, 2021

Write It Out & Meditate...

Hebrews 12:10

_____

_____

_____

_____

_____

Talk to God...

_____

_____

_____

_____

_____

_____

_____

_____

_____

_____

_____

God loves you MORE!

What "SUNSHINE" did you experience today?

_____

_____

_____

_____

_____

_____

_____

_____

_____

_____

_____

_____

_____

_____

_____

_____

_____

_____

_____

_____

Sunshine Loves You!

Write It Out & Meditate...

Matthew 7:1-2

_____

_____

_____

_____

_____

Talk to God...

_____

_____

_____

_____

_____

_____

_____

_____

_____

_____

_____

God loves you MORE!

What "SUNSHINE" did you experience today?

_____

_____

_____

_____

_____

_____

_____

_____

_____

_____

_____

_____

_____

_____

_____

_____

_____

_____

_____

Sunshine Loves You!

April 7, 2021

Write It Out & Meditate...

1st John 3:2

_____

_____

_____

_____

_____

Talk to God...

_____

_____

_____

_____

_____

_____

_____

_____

_____

_____

_____

God loves you MORE!

What "SUNSHINE" did you experience today?

_____

_____

_____

_____

_____

_____

_____

_____

_____

_____

_____

_____

_____

_____

_____

_____

_____

_____

Sunshine Loves You!

Write It Out & Meditate...

1st Peter 2:2-3

_____

_____

_____

_____

_____

Talk to God...

_____

_____

_____

_____

_____

_____

_____

_____

_____

_____

God loves you MORE!

What "SUNSHINE" did you experience today?

_____

_____

_____

_____

_____

_____

_____

_____

_____

_____

_____

_____

_____

_____

_____

_____

_____

_____

_____

Sunshine Loves You!

April 9, 2021

Write It Out & Meditate...

John 3:16

_____

_____

_____

_____

_____

Talk to God...

_____

_____

_____

_____

_____

_____

_____

_____

_____

_____

_____

God loves you MORE!

What "SUNSHINE" did you experience today?

_____

_____

_____

_____

_____

_____

_____

_____

_____

_____

_____

_____

_____

_____

_____

_____

_____

_____

_____

_____

Sunshine Loves You!

Write It Out & Meditate...

Exodus 14:13

_____
_____
_____
_____
_____

Talk to God...

_____
_____
_____
_____
_____
_____
_____
_____
_____
_____
_____

God loves you MORE!

What "SUNSHINE" did you experience today?

_____

_____

_____

_____

_____

_____

_____

_____

_____

_____

_____

_____

_____

_____

_____

_____

_____

_____

_____

Sunshine Loves You!

April 11, 2021

Write It Out & Meditate...

1st Thessalonians 4:16-17

_____

_____

_____

_____

_____

Talk to God...

_____

_____

_____

_____

_____

_____

_____

_____

_____

_____

God loves you MORE!

What "SUNSHINE" did you experience today?

_____

_____

_____

_____

_____

_____

_____

_____

_____

_____

_____

_____

_____

_____

_____

_____

_____

_____

_____

_____

Sunshine Loves You!

Write It Out & Meditate...

2nd Chronicles 7:14

_____

_____

_____

_____

_____

Talk to God...

_____

_____

_____

_____

_____

_____

_____

_____

_____

_____

God loves you MORE!

What "SUNSHINE" did you experience today?

_____

_____

_____

_____

_____

_____

_____

_____

_____

_____

_____

_____

_____

_____

_____

_____

_____

Sunshine Loves You!

Write It Out & Meditate...

1st John 3:9

_____

_____

_____

_____

_____

Talk to God...

_____

_____

_____

_____

_____

_____

_____

_____

_____

_____

_____

God loves you MORE!

What "SUNSHINE" did you experience today?

_____

_____

_____

_____

_____

_____

_____

_____

_____

_____

_____

_____

_____

_____

_____

_____

_____

_____

Sunshine Loves You!

Write It Out & Meditate...

Psalm 119:165

_____

_____

_____

_____

_____

Talk to God...

_____

_____

_____

_____

_____

_____

_____

_____

_____

_____

_____

God loves you MORE!

What "SUNSHINE" did you experience today?

_____

_____

_____

_____

_____

_____

_____

_____

_____

_____

_____

_____

_____

_____

_____

_____

_____

_____

Sunshine Loves You!

April 15, 2021

Write It Out & Meditate...

2nd Samuel 22:4

_____
_____
_____
_____
_____

Talk to God...

_____
_____
_____
_____
_____
_____
_____
_____
_____
_____
_____

God loves you MORE!

What "SUNSHINE" did you experience today?

_____

_____

_____

_____

_____

_____

_____

_____

_____

_____

_____

_____

_____

_____

_____

_____

_____

_____

_____

Sunshine Loves You!

Write It Out & Meditate...

John 3:36

_____

_____

_____

_____

_____

Talk to God...

_____

_____

_____

_____

_____

_____

_____

_____

_____

_____

_____

God loves you MORE!

What "SUNSHINE" did you experience today?

_____

_____

_____

_____

_____

_____

_____

_____

_____

_____

_____

_____

_____

_____

_____

_____

_____

_____

_____

_____

Sunshine Loves You!

April 17, 2021

Write It Out & Meditate...

John 8:36

_____
_____
_____
_____
_____

Talk to God...

_____
_____
_____
_____
_____
_____
_____
_____
_____
_____
_____

God loves you MORE!

What "SUNSHINE" did you experience today?

_____

_____

_____

_____

_____

_____

_____

_____

_____

_____

_____

_____

_____

_____

_____

_____

_____

_____

_____

Sunshine Loves You!

Write It Out & Meditate...

Psalm 16:8

_____

_____

_____

_____

_____

Talk to God...

_____

_____

_____

_____

_____

_____

_____

_____

_____

_____

God loves you MORE!

What "SUNSHINE" did you experience today?

_____

_____

_____

_____

_____

_____

_____

_____

_____

_____

_____

_____

_____

_____

_____

_____

_____

_____

_____

Sunshine Loves You!

Write It Out & Meditate...

James 1:12

_____

_____

_____

_____

_____

Talk to God...

_____

_____

_____

_____

_____

_____

_____

_____

_____

_____

God loves you MORE!

What "SUNSHINE" did you experience today?

_____

_____

_____

_____

_____

_____

_____

_____

_____

_____

_____

_____

_____

_____

_____

_____

_____

_____

Sunshine Loves You!

Write It Out & Meditate...

Ephesians 1:4

_____

_____

_____

_____

_____

Talk to God...

_____

_____

_____

_____

_____

_____

_____

_____

_____

_____

God loves you MORE!

What "SUNSHINE" did you experience today?

_____

_____

_____

_____

_____

_____

_____

_____

_____

_____

_____

_____

_____

_____

_____

_____

_____

_____

_____

Sunshine Loves You!

Write It Out & Meditate...

2nd Thessalonians 1:6

_____

_____

_____

_____

_____

Talk to God...

_____

_____

_____

_____

_____

_____

_____

_____

_____

_____

_____

God loves you MORE!

What "SUNSHINE" did you experience today?

_____

_____

_____

_____

_____

_____

_____

_____

_____

_____

_____

_____

_____

_____

_____

_____

_____

_____

Sunshine Loves You!

Write It Out & Meditate...

Psalm 37:40

_____

_____

_____

_____

_____

Talk to God...

_____

_____

_____

_____

_____

_____

_____

_____

_____

_____

God loves you MORE!

What "SUNSHINE" did you experience today?

_____

_____

_____

_____

_____

_____

_____

_____

_____

_____

_____

_____

_____

_____

_____

_____

_____

_____

Sunshine Loves You!

Write It Out & Meditate...

Malachi 3:10

_____

_____

_____

_____

_____

Talk to God...

_____

_____

_____

_____

_____

_____

_____

_____

_____

_____

_____

God loves you MORE!

What "SUNSHINE" did you experience today?

_____

_____

_____

_____

_____

_____

_____

_____

_____

_____

_____

_____

_____

_____

_____

_____

_____

_____

Sunshine Loves You!

April 24, 2021

Write It Out & Meditate...

Jeremiah 15:19

_____
_____
_____
_____
_____

Talk to God...

_____
_____
_____
_____
_____
_____
_____
_____
_____
_____
_____

God loves you MORE!

What "SUNSHINE" did you experience today?

_____

_____

_____

_____

_____

_____

_____

_____

_____

_____

_____

_____

_____

_____

_____

_____

Sunshine Loves You!

April 25, 2021

Write It Out & Meditate...

Mark 11:24

_____
_____
_____
_____
_____

Talk to God...

_____
_____
_____
_____
_____
_____
_____
_____
_____
_____
_____

God loves you MORE!

What "SUNSHINE" did you experience today?

_____

_____

_____

_____

_____

_____

_____

_____

_____

_____

_____

_____

_____

_____

_____

_____

_____

_____

_____

Sunshine Loves You!

Write It Out & Meditate...

John 1:12-13

_____

_____

_____

_____

_____

Talk to God...

_____

_____

_____

_____

_____

_____

_____

_____

_____

_____

God loves you MORE!

What "SUNSHINE" did you experience today?

_____

_____

_____

_____

_____

_____

_____

_____

_____

_____

_____

_____

_____

_____

_____

_____

_____

_____

Sunshine Loves You!

Write It Out & Meditate...

Joshua 1:9

_____

_____

_____

_____

_____

Talk to God...

_____

_____

_____

_____

_____

_____

_____

_____

_____

_____

_____

_____

God loves you MORE!

What "SUNSHINE" did you experience today?

_____

_____

_____

_____

_____

_____

_____

_____

_____

_____

_____

_____

_____

_____

_____

_____

_____

_____

_____

Sunshine Loves You!

Write It Out & Meditate...

Psalm 18:3

_____

_____

_____

_____

_____

Talk to God...

_____

_____

_____

_____

_____

_____

_____

_____

_____

_____

_____

God loves you MORE!

What "SUNSHINE" did you experience today?

_____

_____

_____

_____

_____

_____

_____

_____

_____

_____

_____

_____

_____

_____

_____

_____

_____

_____

Sunshine Loves You!

Write It Out & Meditate...

John 11:25-26

_____

_____

_____

_____

_____

Talk to God...

_____

_____

_____

_____

_____

_____

_____

_____

_____

_____

God loves you MORE!

What "SUNSHINE" did you experience today?

_____

_____

_____

_____

_____

_____

_____

_____

_____

_____

_____

_____

_____

_____

_____

_____

_____

_____

Sunshine Loves You!

Write It Out & Meditate...

1st Thessalonians 4:13-14

_____

_____

_____

_____

_____

Talk to God...

_____

_____

_____

_____

_____

_____

_____

_____

_____

_____

God loves you MORE!

What "SUNSHINE" did you experience today?

_____

_____

_____

_____

_____

_____

_____

_____

_____

_____

_____

_____

_____

_____

_____

_____

_____

_____

Sunshine Loves You!

May's

Scripture Focus

Let us not become weary in doing good, for at the proper time we will reap a harvest if we do not give up.

Galatians 6:9 NIV

My thoughts about this Scripture:

_____

_____

_____

_____

_____

_____

_____

_____

God loves you MORE!

Sunshine Loves You!

May's
Reflection & Prayer

This is a GREAT MONTH to recognize time as a gift from God. Begin to appreciate every second, every moment of your life. Despite the fact that it seems as though you may be putting out more than you are receiving, continue to sow. Continue to sow your seeds of kindness. Continue to sow your seeds of patience. Continue to sow your seeds of faithfulness. Continue to sow your seeds of gentleness. Continue to sow your seeds of love. Continue to sow your seeds of joy. Someone's time has already expired, but you have been given more time to continue to sow. God sees you sowing through your tears and through your own struggles. He has not forgotten about you. Remain faithful to sowing seeds and doing good solely to please God and not man. Your bountiful harvest is coming forth from the One who gave you the seed. Thank God in advance for the harvest and always remember: you reap what you sow, you reap later than you sow, but you always reap more than you sow. Wait in expectation. It's blooming season.

Father, I thank you that you see all and you know all. You know I get tired sometimes and you also know that I want to give up often times. I am asking that you continue to remind me that none of my labor is in vain. Help me to continue to do everything I do before an audience of one…YOU. Thank you for the seeds that I am planting, for I know that in due season, a bountiful harvest will come forth. When the harvest does come forth, help me to remain humble and to continue to give thanks to you. Thank you in advance for the wherewithal to keep planting seeds and waiting patiently on my harvest.

In Jesus' Name,

AMEN.

God loves you MORE!

May 2021 (United States)

June 2021

S	M	T	W	T	F	S
		1	2	3	4	5
6	7	8	9	10	11	12
13	14	15	16	17	18	19
20	21	22	23	24	25	26
27	28	29	30			

Sun	Mon	Tue	Wed	Thu	Fri	Sat
25	26 ○ Full Moon	27	28	29	30	1
2	3 ☽ 3rd Quarter	4	5 Cinco de Mayo	6	7	8
9 Mother's Day	10	11 ● New Moon	12	13	14	15
16	17	18	19 ☽ 1st Quarter	20	21	22
23	24	25	26 ○ Full Moon	27	28	29
30	31 ● Memorial Day	1	2 ☽ 1st Quarter	3	4	5

● Federal Holidays   ● Local Holidays   ●● Multiple Events

Sunshine Loves You!

Write It Out & Meditate...

Psalm 27:1

_____

_____

_____

_____

_____

Talk to God...

_____

_____

_____

_____

_____

_____

_____

_____

_____

_____

God loves you MORE!

What "SUNSHINE" did you experience today?

_____

_____

_____

_____

_____

_____

_____

_____

_____

_____

_____

_____

_____

_____

_____

_____

_____

_____

_____

Sunshine Loves You!

May 2, 2021

Write It Out & Meditate...

1st Thessalonians 4:13-14

_____
_____
_____
_____
_____

Talk to God...

_____
_____
_____
_____
_____
_____
_____
_____
_____
_____
_____

God loves you MORE!

What "SUNSHINE" did you experience today?

_____

_____

_____

_____

_____

_____

_____

_____

_____

_____

_____

_____

_____

_____

_____

_____

_____

_____

_____

Sunshine Loves You!

May 2, 2021

Write It Out & Meditate...

Philippians 4:13

_____
_____
_____
_____
_____

Talk to God...

_____
_____
_____
_____
_____
_____
_____
_____
_____
_____
_____

God loves you MORE!

What "SUNSHINE" did you experience today?

_____

_____

_____

_____

_____

_____

_____

_____

_____

_____

_____

_____

_____

_____

_____

_____

_____

_____

Sunshine Loves You!

Write It Out & Meditate...

2nd Corinthians 5:21

_____

_____

_____

_____

_____

Talk to God...

_____

_____

_____

_____

_____

_____

_____

_____

_____

_____

God loves you MORE!

What "SUNSHINE" did you experience today?

_____

_____

_____

_____

_____

_____

_____

_____

_____

_____

_____

_____

_____

_____

_____

_____

_____

_____

Sunshine Loves You!

May 4, 2021

Write It Out & Meditate...

Matthew 19:26

_____
_____
_____
_____
_____

Talk to God...

_____
_____
_____
_____
_____
_____
_____
_____
_____
_____
_____

God loves you MORE!

What "SUNSHINE" did you experience today?

_____

_____

_____

_____

_____

_____

_____

_____

_____

_____

_____

_____

_____

_____

_____

_____

_____

_____

_____

Sunshine Loves You!

May 5, 2021

Write It Out & Meditate...

Psalm 16:2

_____
_____
_____
_____
_____

Talk to God...

_____
_____
_____
_____
_____
_____
_____
_____
_____
_____
_____

God loves you MORE!

What "SUNSHINE" did you experience today?

_____

_____

_____

_____

_____

_____

_____

_____

_____

_____

_____

_____

_____

_____

_____

_____

_____

Sunshine Loves You!

Write It Out & Meditate...

Jeremiah 17:10

_____

_____

_____

_____

_____

Talk to God...

_____

_____

_____

_____

_____

_____

_____

_____

_____

_____

God loves you MORE!

What "SUNSHINE" did you experience today?

_____

_____

_____

_____

_____

_____

_____

_____

_____

_____

_____

_____

_____

_____

_____

_____

_____

_____

Sunshine Loves You!

May 7, 2021

Write It Out & Meditate...

Colossians 3:4

_____
_____
_____
_____
_____

Talk to God...

_____
_____
_____
_____
_____
_____
_____
_____
_____
_____

God loves you MORE!

What "SUNSHINE" did you experience today?

_____

_____

_____

_____

_____

_____

_____

_____

_____

_____

_____

_____

_____

_____

_____

_____

_____

_____

_____

_____

Sunshine Loves You!

Write It Out & Meditate...

2nd Corinthians 4:16

_____

_____

_____

_____

_____

Talk to God...

_____

_____

_____

_____

_____

_____

_____

_____

_____

_____

_____

God loves you MORE!

What "SUNSHINE" did you experience today?

_____

_____

_____

_____

_____

_____

_____

_____

_____

_____

_____

_____

_____

_____

_____

_____

_____

Sunshine Loves You!

Write It Out & Meditate...

James 4:10

_____
_____
_____
_____
_____

Talk to God...

_____
_____
_____
_____
_____
_____
_____
_____
_____
_____

God loves you MORE!

What "SUNSHINE" did you experience today?

_____

_____

_____

_____

_____

_____

_____

_____

_____

_____

_____

_____

_____

_____

_____

_____

_____

_____

_____

_____

_____

Sunshine Loves You!

May 10, 2021

Write It Out & Meditate...

Jeremiah 32:27

_____
_____
_____
_____
_____

Talk to God...

_____
_____
_____
_____
_____
_____
_____
_____
_____
_____
_____

God loves you MORE!

What "SUNSHINE" did you experience today?

_____

_____

_____

_____

_____

_____

_____

_____

_____

_____

_____

_____

_____

_____

_____

_____

_____

_____

Sunshine Loves You!

Write It Out & Meditate...

Psalm 55:22

_____

_____

_____

_____

_____

Talk to God...

_____

_____

_____

_____

_____

_____

_____

_____

_____

_____

_____

God loves you MORE!

What "SUNSHINE" did you experience today?

_____

_____

_____

_____

_____

_____

_____

_____

_____

_____

_____

_____

_____

_____

_____

_____

_____

_____

_____

Sunshine Loves You!

Write It Out & Meditate...

Psalm 34:17

_____

_____

_____

_____

_____

Talk to God...

_____

_____

_____

_____

_____

_____

_____

_____

_____

_____

_____

God loves you MORE!

What "SUNSHINE" did you experience today?

_____

_____

_____

_____

_____

_____

_____

_____

_____

_____

_____

_____

_____

_____

_____

_____

_____

_____

_____

Sunshine Loves You!

Write It Out & Meditate...

Jeremiah 29:13

_____

_____

_____

_____

_____

Talk to God...

_____

_____

_____

_____

_____

_____

_____

_____

_____

_____

_____

God loves you MORE!

What "SUNSHINE" did you experience today?

_____

_____

_____

_____

_____

_____

_____

_____

_____

_____

_____

_____

_____

_____

_____

_____

_____

_____

_____

Sunshine Loves You!

Write It Out & Meditate...

Ezekiel 34:31

_____

_____

_____

_____

_____

Talk to God...

_____

_____

_____

_____

_____

_____

_____

_____

_____

_____

_____

God loves you MORE!

What "SUNSHINE" did you experience today?

_____

_____

_____

_____

_____

_____

_____

_____

_____

_____

_____

_____

_____

_____

_____

_____

_____

_____

Sunshine Loves You!

Write It Out & Meditate...

Psalm 37:4

_____

_____

_____

_____

_____

Talk to God...

_____

_____

_____

_____

_____

_____

_____

_____

_____

_____

_____

God loves you MORE!

What "SUNSHINE" did you experience today?

_____

_____

_____

_____

_____

_____

_____

_____

_____

_____

_____

_____

_____

_____

_____

_____

_____

_____

_____

_____

Sunshine Loves You!

Write It Out & Meditate...

Isaiah 43:1

_____

_____

_____

_____

_____

Talk to God...

_____

_____

_____

_____

_____

_____

_____

_____

_____

_____

_____

God loves you MORE!

What "SUNSHINE" did you experience today?

_____

_____

_____

_____

_____

_____

_____

_____

_____

_____

_____

_____

_____

_____

_____

_____

_____

_____

Sunshine Loves You!

Write It Out & Meditate...

2nd Thessalonians 3:3

_____

_____

_____

_____

_____

Talk to God...

_____

_____

_____

_____

_____

_____

_____

_____

_____

_____

God loves you MORE!

What "SUNSHINE" did you experience today?

_____

_____

_____

_____

_____

_____

_____

_____

_____

_____

_____

_____

_____

_____

_____

_____

_____

_____

_____

Sunshine Loves You!

Write It Out & Meditate...

Psalm 145:18

_____
_____
_____
_____
_____

Talk to God...

_____
_____
_____
_____
_____
_____
_____
_____
_____
_____
_____

God loves you MORE!

What "SUNSHINE" did you experience today?

_____

_____

_____

_____

_____

_____

_____

_____

_____

_____

_____

_____

_____

_____

_____

_____

_____

_____

Sunshine Loves You!

Write It Out & Meditate...

Psalm 86:5

_____

_____

_____

_____

_____

Talk to God...

_____

_____

_____

_____

_____

_____

_____

_____

_____

_____

_____

God loves you MORE!

What "SUNSHINE" did you experience today?

_____

_____

_____

_____

_____

_____

_____

_____

_____

_____

_____

_____

_____

_____

_____

_____

_____

_____

_____

Sunshine Loves You!

Write It Out & Meditate...

1st John 5:11-12

_____

_____

_____

_____

_____

Talk to God...

_____

_____

_____

_____

_____

_____

_____

_____

_____

_____

_____

God loves you MORE!

What "SUNSHINE" did you experience today?

_____

_____

_____

_____

_____

_____

_____

_____

_____

_____

_____

_____

_____

_____

_____

_____

_____

_____

Sunshine Loves You!

Write It Out & Meditate...

Deuteronomy 4:29

_____

_____

_____

_____

_____

Talk to God...

_____

_____

_____

_____

_____

_____

_____

_____

_____

_____

_____

God loves you MORE!

What "SUNSHINE" did you experience today?

_____

_____

_____

_____

_____

_____

_____

_____

_____

_____

_____

_____

_____

_____

_____

_____

_____

_____

Sunshine Loves You!

Write It Out & Meditate...

Proverbs 13:11

_____

_____

_____

_____

_____

Talk to God...

_____

_____

_____

_____

_____

_____

_____

_____

_____

_____

_____

God loves you MORE!

What "SUNSHINE" did you experience today?

_____

_____

_____

_____

_____

_____

_____

_____

_____

_____

_____

_____

_____

_____

_____

_____

_____

_____

Sunshine Loves You!

Write It Out & Meditate...

Romans 8:38-39

_____

_____

_____

_____

_____

Talk to God...

_____

_____

_____

_____

_____

_____

_____

_____

_____

_____

_____

God loves you MORE!

What "SUNSHINE" did you experience today?

_____

_____

_____

_____

_____

_____

_____

_____

_____

_____

_____

_____

_____

_____

_____

_____

_____

Sunshine Loves You!

Write It Out & Meditate...

Psalm 63:8

_____

_____

_____

_____

_____

Talk to God...

_____

_____

_____

_____

_____

_____

_____

_____

_____

_____

_____

God loves you MORE!

What "SUNSHINE" did you experience today?

_____

_____

_____

_____

_____

_____

_____

_____

_____

_____

_____

_____

_____

_____

_____

_____

_____

Sunshine Loves You!

Write It Out & Meditate...

Mark 12:30

_____

_____

_____

_____

_____

Talk to God...

_____

_____

_____

_____

_____

_____

_____

_____

_____

_____

_____

God loves you MORE!

What "SUNSHINE" did you experience today?

_____

_____

_____

_____

_____

_____

_____

_____

_____

_____

_____

_____

_____

_____

_____

_____

_____

_____

Sunshine Loves You!

Write It Out & Meditate...

Genesis 17:7

_____

_____

_____

_____

_____

Talk to God...

_____

_____

_____

_____

_____

_____

_____

_____

_____

_____

_____

God loves you MORE!

What "SUNSHINE" did you experience today?

_____

_____

_____

_____

_____

_____

_____

_____

_____

_____

_____

_____

_____

_____

_____

_____

_____

_____

_____

Sunshine Loves You!

Write It Out & Meditate...

Titus 3:4-5

_____
_____
_____
_____
_____

Talk to God...

_____
_____
_____
_____
_____
_____
_____
_____
_____
_____
_____

God loves you MORE!

What "SUNSHINE" did you experience today?

_____

_____

_____

_____

_____

_____

_____

_____

_____

_____

_____

_____

_____

_____

_____

_____

_____

_____

_____

_____

Sunshine Loves You!

Write It Out & Meditate...

Proverbs 22:6

_____
_____
_____
_____
_____

Talk to God...

_____
_____
_____
_____
_____
_____
_____
_____
_____
_____
_____

God loves you MORE!

What "SUNSHINE" did you experience today?

_____

_____

_____

_____

_____

_____

_____

_____

_____

_____

_____

_____

_____

_____

_____

_____

_____

_____

Sunshine Loves You!

Write It Out & Meditate...

Revelation 3:5

_____

_____

_____

_____

_____

Talk to God...

_____

_____

_____

_____

_____

_____

_____

_____

_____

_____

God loves you MORE!

What "SUNSHINE" did you experience today?

_____

_____

_____

_____

_____

_____

_____

_____

_____

_____

_____

_____

_____

_____

_____

_____

_____

_____

_____

Sunshine Loves You!

May 30, 2021

Write It Out & Meditate...

Deuteronomy 23:14

_____
_____
_____
_____
_____

Talk to God...

_____
_____
_____
_____
_____
_____
_____
_____
_____
_____
_____

God loves you MORE!

What "SUNSHINE" did you experience today?

_____

_____

_____

_____

_____

_____

_____

_____

_____

_____

_____

_____

_____

_____

_____

_____

_____

_____

Sunshine Loves You!

Write It Out & Meditate...

Psalm 54:4

_____

_____

_____

_____

_____

Talk to God...

_____

_____

_____

_____

_____

_____

_____

_____

_____

_____

_____

God loves you MORE!

What "SUNSHINE" did you experience today?

_____

_____

_____

_____

_____

_____

_____

_____

_____

_____

_____

_____

_____

_____

_____

_____

_____

_____

Sunshine Loves You!

June's
Scripture Focus

When you pass through the waters, I will be with you; and when you pass through the rivers, they will not sweep over you. When you walk through the fire, you will not be burned; the flames will not set you ablaze.

Isaiah 43:2 NIV

My thoughts about this Scripture:

_____

_____

_____

_____

_____

_____

_____

God loves you MORE!

Sunshine Loves You!

June's
Reflection & Prayer

This is a GREAT MONTH to follow the Master's direction. Get out of the driver's seat and let God drive you to His Will and to your destiny. No more being the Pilot. Switch seats with God and let him fully take over your life. Be content and acknowledge that God knows best. Quiet your life this month. Be intentional and make time for God. Stop overtalking God and learn to listen. Remember, God speaks through His Word, through songs and through other people. God speaks in a variety of ways. Slow down. Be quiet. Listen. Have an open state of mind. God has your best interest at hand and His answer may not always be what you want to hear, but it will always be what you need to hear.

Father, I thank you that you are an omnipresent and omnipotent God. God, forgive me for trying to do things my own way. I'm removing myself from the driver's seat, putting myself back in my rightful position in the passenger's seat and giving you the keys and permission to take over this ride. You know my destiny and the destination you are trying to get me to. I know I'm going to experience a few speed bumps, a few potholes and a few traffic stops on this journey called Life, but I know that you as my chauffeur, will get me to my destination safe and sound. I'm ready for the ride God. Help me to enjoy it, learn from the experiences along the way and help me not to grumble, take my seat belt off and cause my own fatality. I trust you God. Let's ride out.

In Jesus' Name,

AMEN.

God loves you MORE!

June 2021 (United States)

July 2021
S M T W T F S
1 2 3
4 5 6 7 8 9 10
11 12 13 14 15 16 17
18 19 20 21 22 23 24
25 26 27 28 29 30 31

Sun	Mon	Tue	Wed	Thu	Fri	Sat
30	31 Memorial Day	1	2 ◑ 3rd Quarter	3	4	5
6	7	8	9	10 ● New Moon	11	12
13	14	15	16	17 ◐ 1st Quarter	18	19 Juneteenth
20 Father's Day	21	22	23	24 ○ Full Moon	25	26
27	28	29	30	1 ◑ 3rd Quarter	2	3

● Federal Holidays   ● Local Holidays   ●) Religious Events

Sunshine Loves You!

Write It Out & Meditate...

Deuteronomy 4:40

_____

_____

_____

_____

_____

Talk to God...

_____

_____

_____

_____

_____

_____

_____

_____

_____

_____

God loves you MORE!

What "SUNSHINE" did you experience today?

_____

_____

_____

_____

_____

_____

_____

_____

_____

_____

_____

_____

_____

_____

_____

_____

_____

_____

_____

_____

Sunshine Loves You!

Write It Out & Meditate...

Hebrews 6:10

_____

_____

_____

_____

_____

Talk to God...

_____

_____

_____

_____

_____

_____

_____

_____

_____

_____

God loves you MORE!

What "SUNSHINE" did you experience today?

_____

_____

_____

_____

_____

_____

_____

_____

_____

_____

_____

_____

_____

_____

_____

_____

_____

_____

Sunshine Loves You!

Write It Out & Meditate...

Psalm 37:5-6

_____

_____

_____

_____

_____

Talk to God...

_____

_____

_____

_____

_____

_____

_____

_____

_____

_____

_____

God loves you MORE!

What "SUNSHINE" did you experience today?

_____

_____

_____

_____

_____

_____

_____

_____

_____

_____

_____

_____

_____

_____

_____

_____

_____

_____

Sunshine Loves You!

Write It Out & Meditate...

Psalm 84:11

_____

_____

_____

_____

_____

Talk to God...

_____

_____

_____

_____

_____

_____

_____

_____

_____

_____

_____

God loves you MORE!

What "SUNSHINE" did you experience today?

_____

_____

_____

_____

_____

_____

_____

_____

_____

_____

_____

_____

_____

_____

_____

_____

_____

_____

_____

Sunshine Loves You!

Write It Out & Meditate...

Romans 8:18

_____

_____

_____

_____

_____

Talk to God...

_____

_____

_____

_____

_____

_____

_____

_____

_____

_____

_____

God loves you MORE!

What "SUNSHINE" did you experience today?

_____

_____

_____

_____

_____

_____

_____

_____

_____

_____

_____

_____

_____

_____

_____

_____

_____

Sunshine Loves You!

Write It Out & Meditate...

Psalm 9:9

_____

_____

_____

_____

_____

Talk to God...

_____

_____

_____

_____

_____

_____

_____

_____

_____

_____

_____

God loves you MORE!

What "SUNSHINE" did you experience today?

_____

_____

_____

_____

_____

_____

_____

_____

_____

_____

_____

_____

_____

_____

_____

_____

_____

_____

Sunshine Loves You!

June 7, 2021

Write It Out & Meditate...

1st John 5:14-15

_____
_____
_____
_____
_____

Talk to God...

_____
_____
_____
_____
_____
_____
_____
_____
_____

God loves you MORE!

What "SUNSHINE" did you experience today?

_____

_____

_____

_____

_____

_____

_____

_____

_____

_____

_____

_____

_____

_____

_____

_____

_____

_____

_____

Sunshine Loves You!

Write It Out & Meditate...

Deuteronomy 8:18

_____

_____

_____

_____

_____

Talk to God...

_____

_____

_____

_____

_____

_____

_____

_____

_____

_____

God loves you MORE!

What "SUNSHINE" did you experience today?

_____

_____

_____

_____

_____

_____

_____

_____

_____

_____

_____

_____

_____

_____

_____

_____

_____

_____

Sunshine Loves You!

Write It Out & Meditate...

Ecclesiastes 3:1-8

_____

_____

_____

_____

_____

Talk to God...

_____

_____

_____

_____

_____

_____

_____

_____

_____

_____

_____

God loves you MORE!

What "SUNSHINE" did you experience today?

_____

_____

_____

_____

_____

_____

_____

_____

_____

_____

_____

_____

_____

_____

_____

_____

_____

_____

Sunshine Loves You!

Write It Out & Meditate...

Romans 10:9-10

_____

_____

_____

_____

_____

Talk to God...

_____

_____

_____

_____

_____

_____

_____

_____

_____

_____

_____

God loves you MORE!

What "SUNSHINE" did you experience today?

_____

_____

_____

_____

_____

_____

_____

_____

_____

_____

_____

_____

_____

_____

_____

_____

_____

_____

_____

_____

_____

_____

Sunshine Loves You!

Write It Out & Meditate...

Proverbs 3:5-6

_____

_____

_____

_____

_____

Talk to God...

_____

_____

_____

_____

_____

_____

_____

_____

_____

_____

_____

God loves you MORE!

What "SUNSHINE" did you experience today?

_____

_____

_____

_____

_____

_____

_____

_____

_____

_____

_____

_____

_____

_____

_____

_____

_____

_____

_____

_____

Sunshine Loves You!

Write It Out & Meditate...

James 5:14-15

_____

_____

_____

_____

_____

Talk to God...

_____

_____

_____

_____

_____

_____

_____

_____

_____

_____

_____

God loves you MORE!

What "SUNSHINE" did you experience today?

_____

_____

_____

_____

_____

_____

_____

_____

_____

_____

_____

_____

_____

_____

_____

_____

_____

_____

_____

Sunshine Loves You!

Write It Out & Meditate...

Psalm 62:1-2

_____
_____
_____
_____
_____

Talk to God...

_____
_____
_____
_____
_____
_____
_____
_____
_____
_____
_____

God loves you MORE!

What "SUNSHINE" did you experience today?

_____

_____

_____

_____

_____

_____

_____

_____

_____

_____

_____

_____

_____

_____

_____

_____

_____

_____

_____

_____

Sunshine Loves You!

Write It Out & Meditate...

Matthew 6:31-32

_____

_____

_____

_____

_____

Talk to God...

_____

_____

_____

_____

_____

_____

_____

_____

_____

_____

_____

God loves you MORE!

What "SUNSHINE" did you experience today?

_____

_____

_____

_____

_____

_____

_____

_____

_____

_____

_____

_____

_____

_____

_____

_____

_____

_____

Sunshine Loves You!

Write It Out & Meditate...

Matthew 7:9-11

_____

_____

_____

_____

_____

Talk to God...

_____

_____

_____

_____

_____

_____

_____

_____

_____

_____

God loves you MORE!

What "SUNSHINE" did you experience today?

_____

_____

_____

_____

_____

_____

_____

_____

_____

_____

_____

_____

_____

_____

_____

_____

_____

_____

Sunshine Loves You!

Write It Out & Meditate...

Psalm 50:15

_____

_____

_____

_____

_____

Talk to God...

_____

_____

_____

_____

_____

_____

_____

_____

_____

_____

_____

God loves you MORE!

What "SUNSHINE" did you experience today?

_____

_____

_____

_____

_____

_____

_____

_____

_____

_____

_____

_____

_____

_____

_____

_____

_____

_____

_____

_____

Sunshine Loves You!

Write It Out & Meditate...

James 4:8

_____

_____

_____

_____

_____

Talk to God...

_____

_____

_____

_____

_____

_____

_____

_____

_____

_____

_____

God loves you MORE!

What "SUNSHINE" did you experience today?

_____

_____

_____

_____

_____

_____

_____

_____

_____

_____

_____

_____

_____

_____

_____

_____

_____

_____

_____

_____

_____

_____

Sunshine Loves You!

Write It Out & Meditate...

Psalm 103:2-5

_____

_____

_____

_____

_____

Talk to God...

_____

_____

_____

_____

_____

_____

_____

_____

_____

_____

God loves you MORE!

What "SUNSHINE" did you experience today?

_____

_____

_____

_____

_____

_____

_____

_____

_____

_____

_____

_____

_____

_____

_____

_____

_____

_____

_____

_____

Sunshine Loves You!

June 19, 2021

Write It Out & Meditate...

John 14:12

_____
_____
_____
_____
_____

Talk to God...

_____
_____
_____
_____
_____
_____
_____
_____
_____
_____
_____

God loves you MORE!

What "SUNSHINE" did you experience today?

_____

_____

_____

_____

_____

_____

_____

_____

_____

_____

_____

_____

_____

_____

_____

_____

_____

_____

Sunshine Loves You!

June 20, 2021

Write It Out & Meditate...

Jeremiah 31:25

_____
_____
_____
_____
_____

Talk to God...

_____
_____
_____
_____
_____
_____
_____
_____
_____
_____

God loves you MORE!

What "SUNSHINE" did you experience today?

_____

_____

_____

_____

_____

_____

_____

_____

_____

_____

_____

_____

_____

_____

_____

_____

_____

_____

_____

Sunshine Loves You!

June 21, 2021

Write It Out & Meditate...

2nd Corinthians 6:18

_____
_____
_____
_____
_____

Talk to God...

_____
_____
_____
_____
_____
_____
_____
_____
_____
_____

God loves you MORE!

What "SUNSHINE" did you experience today?

_____

_____

_____

_____

_____

_____

_____

_____

_____

_____

_____

_____

_____

_____

_____

_____

_____

_____

_____

_____

Sunshine Loves You!

June 22, 2021

Write It Out & Meditate...

Galatians 6:9

_____
_____
_____
_____
_____

Talk to God...

_____
_____
_____
_____
_____
_____
_____
_____
_____
_____

God loves you MORE!

What "SUNSHINE" did you experience today?

_____

_____

_____

_____

_____

_____

_____

_____

_____

_____

_____

_____

_____

_____

_____

_____

_____

_____

Sunshine Loves You!

June 23, 2021

Write It Out & Meditate...

Psalm 37:7

_____
_____
_____
_____
_____

Talk to God...

_____
_____
_____
_____
_____
_____
_____
_____
_____
_____
_____

God loves you MORE!

What "SUNSHINE" did you experience today?

_____

_____

_____

_____

_____

_____

_____

_____

_____

_____

_____

_____

_____

_____

_____

_____

_____

_____

Sunshine Loves You!

Write It Out & Meditate...

Psalm 107:13-16

_____

_____

_____

_____

_____

Talk to God...

_____

_____

_____

_____

_____

_____

_____

_____

_____

_____

_____

God loves you MORE!

What "SUNSHINE" did you experience today?

_____

_____

_____

_____

_____

_____

_____

_____

_____

_____

_____

_____

_____

_____

_____

_____

_____

_____

_____

Sunshine Loves You!

June 25, 2021

Write It Out & Meditate...

1st Corinthians 11:32

_____
_____
_____
_____
_____

Talk to God...

_____
_____
_____
_____
_____
_____
_____
_____
_____
_____
_____

God loves you MORE!

What "SUNSHINE" did you experience today?

_____

_____

_____

_____

_____

_____

_____

_____

_____

_____

_____

_____

_____

_____

_____

_____

_____

Sunshine Loves You!

June 26, 2021

Write It Out & Meditate...

Deuteronomy 28:13

_____
_____
_____
_____
_____

Talk to God...

_____
_____
_____
_____
_____
_____
_____
_____
_____
_____
_____
_____

God loves you MORE!

What "SUNSHINE" did you experience today?

_____

_____

_____

_____

_____

_____

_____

_____

_____

_____

_____

_____

_____

_____

_____

_____

_____

Sunshine Loves You!

Write It Out & Meditate...

Jeremiah 1:5

_____

_____

_____

_____

_____

Talk to God...

_____

_____

_____

_____

_____

_____

_____

_____

_____

_____

_____

God loves you MORE!

What "SUNSHINE" did you experience today?

_____

_____

_____

_____

_____

_____

_____

_____

_____

_____

_____

_____

_____

_____

_____

_____

_____

_____

_____

Sunshine Loves You!

Write It Out & Meditate...

Isaiah 30:21

_____

_____

_____

_____

_____

Talk to God...

_____

_____

_____

_____

_____

_____

_____

_____

_____

_____

_____

God loves you MORE!

What "SUNSHINE" did you experience today?

_____

_____

_____

_____

_____

_____

_____

_____

_____

_____

_____

_____

_____

_____

_____

_____

_____

_____

_____

_____

Sunshine Loves You!

Write It Out & Meditate...

John 14:15

_____
_____
_____
_____
_____

Talk to God...

_____
_____
_____
_____
_____
_____
_____
_____
_____
_____
_____

God loves you MORE!

What "SUNSHINE" did you experience today?

_____

_____

_____

_____

_____

_____

_____

_____

_____

_____

_____

_____

_____

_____

_____

_____

_____

_____

Sunshine Loves You!

June 30, 2021

Write It Out & Meditate...

1st Peter 5:7

_____
_____
_____
_____
_____

Talk to God...

_____
_____
_____
_____
_____
_____
_____
_____
_____
_____
_____

God loves you MORE!

What "SUNSHINE" did you experience today?

_____

_____

_____

_____

_____

_____

_____

_____

_____

_____

_____

_____

_____

_____

_____

_____

_____

_____

_____

Sunshine Loves You!

July's

Scripture Focus

Consider it pure joy, my brothers and sisters, whenever you face trials of many kinds, because you know that the testing of your faith produces perseverance.

James 1: 2-3 NIV

My thoughts about this Scripture:

_____

_____

_____

_____

_____

_____

_____

God loves you MORE!

Sunshine Loves You!

July's
Reflection & Prayer

This is a GREAT MONTH to face your problems with the understanding that God has hidden a blessing within each problem. It's up to you to discover the hidden gem. Thank God for the trials you endure. Each of these trials are necessary and are molding you into the person God needs you to be for His Kingdom. Remember, diamonds are formed under pressure, but never forget they aren't formed overnight. Go through your process and give God glory for each trial. You're coming out as the beautiful gem God has created you to be. Don't rush the process. God knows you can withstand the heat. Let Him refine you. Let Him mold you. Let Him do His work with and in you so that you can come forth as pure gold.

Father, I thank you for giving me a different perspective on the trials and tribulations that I've had to endure, that I'm currently enduring and even for the future ones I will endure. Please forgive me for grumbling, murmuring and speaking against what you already had designed for me to go through before I was even born. I now know each situation has been used to mold me into the individual you are calling me to be. Help me to always see your hand in everything I go through. Help me to remove my feelings about a situation and to know you are working it all out for my good. Help me to go through my trials giving You the glory. Help me not to look to anyone for sympathy or empathy, but look to You, because all of my help comes from You.

In Jesus' Name,
AMEN.

God loves you MORE!

July 2021 (United States)

August 2021

S	M	T	W	T	F	S
1	2	3	4	5	6	7
8	9	10	11	12	13	14
15	16	17	18	19	20	21
22	23	24	25	26	27	28
29	30	31				

Sun	Mon	Tue	Wed	Thu	Fri	Sat
27	28	29	30	1 ◑ 3rd Quarter	2	3
4 ● Independence Day	5 ● 'Independence Day' observed	6	7	8	9 ● New Moon	10
11	12	13	14	15	16	17 ◐ 1st Quarter
18	19	20	21	22	23 ○ Full Moon	24
25	26	27	28	29	30	31 ◑ 3rd Quarter

● Federal Holidays   ● Local Holidays   ◐ Highlight Events

Sunshine Loves You!

Write It Out & Meditate...

John 14:13

_____
_____
_____
_____
_____

Talk to God...

_____
_____
_____
_____
_____
_____
_____
_____
_____
_____
_____
_____

God loves you MORE!

What "SUNSHINE" did you experience today?

_____

_____

_____

_____

_____

_____

_____

_____

_____

_____

_____

_____

_____

_____

_____

_____

_____

_____

_____

Sunshine Loves You!

Write It Out & Meditate...

Psalm 85:8

_____

_____

_____

_____

_____

Talk to God...

_____

_____

_____

_____

_____

_____

_____

_____

_____

_____

God loves you MORE!

What "SUNSHINE" did you experience today?

_____

_____

_____

_____

_____

_____

_____

_____

_____

_____

_____

_____

_____

_____

_____

_____

_____

_____

_____

_____

Sunshine Loves You!

Write It Out & Meditate...

Matthew 24:35

_____

_____

_____

_____

_____

Talk to God...

_____

_____

_____

_____

_____

_____

_____

_____

_____

_____

_____

God loves you MORE!

What "SUNSHINE" did you experience today?

_____

_____

_____

_____

_____

_____

_____

_____

_____

_____

_____

_____

_____

_____

_____

_____

_____

_____

_____

Sunshine Loves You!

July 4, 2021

Write It Out & Meditate...

Ephesians 3:12

_____

_____

_____

_____

_____

Talk to God...

_____

_____

_____

_____

_____

_____

_____

_____

_____

_____

God loves you MORE!

What "SUNSHINE" did you experience today?

_____

_____

_____

_____

_____

_____

_____

_____

_____

_____

_____

_____

_____

_____

_____

_____

_____

_____

_____

Sunshine Loves You!

July 5, 2021

Write It Out & Meditate...

Romans 8:31

_____
_____
_____
_____
_____

Talk to God...

_____
_____
_____
_____
_____
_____
_____
_____
_____
_____
_____

God loves you MORE!

What "SUNSHINE" did you experience today?

_____

_____

_____

_____

_____

_____

_____

_____

_____

_____

_____

_____

_____

_____

_____

_____

_____

_____

_____

_____

Sunshine Loves You!

July 6, 2021

Write It Out & Meditate...

Psalm 89:34

_____

_____

_____

_____

_____

Talk to God...

_____

_____

_____

_____

_____

_____

_____

_____

_____

_____

_____

God loves you MORE!

What "SUNSHINE" did you experience today?

_____

_____

_____

_____

_____

_____

_____

_____

_____

_____

_____

_____

_____

_____

_____

_____

_____

_____

Sunshine Loves You!

July 7, 2021

Write It Out & Meditate...

1ˢᵗ John 5:18

_____
_____
_____
_____
_____

Talk to God...

_____
_____
_____
_____
_____
_____
_____
_____
_____
_____
_____

God loves you MORE!

What "SUNSHINE" did you experience today?

_____

_____

_____

_____

_____

_____

_____

_____

_____

_____

_____

_____

_____

_____

_____

_____

_____

_____

_____

_____

Sunshine Loves You!

Write It Out & Meditate...

Mark 9:23

_____

_____

_____

_____

_____

Talk to God...

_____

_____

_____

_____

_____

_____

_____

_____

_____

_____

God loves you MORE!

What "SUNSHINE" did you experience today?

_____

_____

_____

_____

_____

_____

_____

_____

_____

_____

_____

_____

_____

_____

_____

_____

_____

_____

Sunshine Loves You!

Write It Out & Meditate...

Romans 8:28

_____

_____

_____

_____

_____

Talk to God...

_____

_____

_____

_____

_____

_____

_____

_____

_____

_____

_____

God loves you MORE!

What "SUNSHINE" did you experience today?

_____

_____

_____

_____

_____

_____

_____

_____

_____

_____

_____

_____

_____

_____

_____

_____

_____

_____

Sunshine Loves You!

Write It Out & Meditate...

Isaiah 65:24

_____

_____

_____

_____

_____

Talk to God...

_____

_____

_____

_____

_____

_____

_____

_____

_____

_____

_____

God loves you MORE!

What "SUNSHINE" did you experience today?

_____

_____

_____

_____

_____

_____

_____

_____

_____

_____

_____

_____

_____

_____

_____

_____

_____

_____

_____

Sunshine Loves You!

Write It Out & Meditate...

Matthew 5:10

_____

_____

_____

_____

_____

Talk to God...

_____

_____

_____

_____

_____

_____

_____

_____

_____

_____

_____

God loves you MORE!

What "SUNSHINE" did you experience today?

_____

_____

_____

_____

_____

_____

_____

_____

_____

_____

_____

_____

_____

_____

_____

_____

_____

_____

_____

_____

Sunshine Loves You!

Write It Out & Meditate...

John 15:16

_____

_____

_____

_____

_____

Talk to God...

_____

_____

_____

_____

_____

_____

_____

_____

_____

_____

God loves you MORE!

What "SUNSHINE" did you experience today?

_____

_____

_____

_____

_____

_____

_____

_____

_____

_____

_____

_____

_____

_____

_____

_____

_____

_____

_____

_____

_____

_____

Sunshine Loves You!

Write It Out & Meditate...

Numbers 23:19

_____

_____

_____

_____

_____

Talk to God...

_____

_____

_____

_____

_____

_____

_____

_____

_____

_____

_____

_____

God loves you MORE!

What "SUNSHINE" did you experience today?

_____

_____

_____

_____

_____

_____

_____

_____

_____

_____

_____

_____

_____

_____

_____

_____

_____

_____

_____

Sunshine Loves You!

Write It Out & Meditate...

Philippians 1:6

_____
_____
_____
_____
_____

Talk to God...

_____
_____
_____
_____
_____
_____
_____
_____
_____
_____
_____

God loves you MORE!

What "SUNSHINE" did you experience today?

_____

_____

_____

_____

_____

_____

_____

_____

_____

_____

_____

_____

_____

_____

_____

_____

_____

_____

_____

_____

Sunshine Loves You!

Write It Out & Meditate...

Matthew 6:19-21

_____

_____

_____

_____

_____

Talk to God...

_____

_____

_____

_____

_____

_____

_____

_____

_____

_____

_____

God loves you MORE!

What "SUNSHINE" did you experience today?

_____

_____

_____

_____

_____

_____

_____

_____

_____

_____

_____

_____

_____

_____

_____

_____

_____

_____

_____

_____

Sunshine Loves You!

July 16, 2021

Write It Out & Meditate...

Psalm 91:9-10

_____
_____
_____
_____
_____

Talk to God...

_____
_____
_____
_____
_____
_____
_____
_____
_____
_____
_____

God loves you MORE!

What "SUNSHINE" did you experience today?

_____

_____

_____

_____

_____

_____

_____

_____

_____

_____

_____

_____

_____

_____

_____

_____

_____

_____

_____

Sunshine Loves You!

Write It Out & Meditate...

Matthew 16:26

_____

_____

_____

_____

_____

Talk to God...

_____

_____

_____

_____

_____

_____

_____

_____

_____

_____

_____

God loves you MORE!

What "SUNSHINE" did you experience today?

_____

_____

_____

_____

_____

_____

_____

_____

_____

_____

_____

_____

_____

_____

_____

_____

_____

_____

Sunshine Loves You!

Write It Out & Meditate...

Exodus 33:14

_____

_____

_____

_____

_____

Talk to God...

_____

_____

_____

_____

_____

_____

_____

_____

_____

_____

_____

God loves you MORE!

What "SUNSHINE" did you experience today?

_____

_____

_____

_____

_____

_____

_____

_____

_____

_____

_____

_____

_____

_____

_____

_____

_____

_____

_____

_____

Sunshine Loves You!

Write It Out & Meditate...

Psalm 145:9

_____

_____

_____

_____

_____

Talk to God...

_____

_____

_____

_____

_____

_____

_____

_____

_____

_____

_____

God loves you MORE!

What "SUNSHINE" did you experience today?

_____

_____

_____

_____

_____

_____

_____

_____

_____

_____

_____

_____

_____

_____

_____

_____

_____

_____

_____

_____

Sunshine Loves You!

July 20, 2021

Write It Out & Meditate...

John 15:7

_____
_____
_____
_____
_____

Talk to God...

_____
_____
_____
_____
_____
_____
_____
_____
_____
_____
_____

God loves you MORE!

What "SUNSHINE" did you experience today?

_____

_____

_____

_____

_____

_____

_____

_____

_____

_____

_____

_____

_____

_____

_____

_____

_____

_____

_____

_____

Sunshine Loves You!

July 21, 2021

Write It Out & Meditate...

2nd Corinthians 4:17

_____
_____
_____
_____
_____

Talk to God...

_____
_____
_____
_____
_____
_____
_____
_____
_____
_____
_____

God loves you MORE!

What "SUNSHINE" did you experience today?

_____

_____

_____

_____

_____

_____

_____

_____

_____

_____

_____

_____

_____

_____

_____

_____

_____

_____

_____

_____

Sunshine Loves You!

July 22, 2021

Write It Out & Meditate...

1st Chronicles 16:34

_____
_____
_____
_____
_____

Talk to God...

_____
_____
_____
_____
_____
_____
_____
_____
_____
_____
_____
_____

God loves you MORE!

What "SUNSHINE" did you experience today?

_____

_____

_____

_____

_____

_____

_____

_____

_____

_____

_____

_____

_____

_____

_____

_____

_____

_____

Sunshine Loves You!

July 23, 2021

Write It Out & Meditate...

Psalm 37:8

_____
_____
_____
_____
_____

Talk to God...

_____
_____
_____
_____
_____
_____
_____
_____
_____
_____
_____

God loves you MORE!

What "SUNSHINE" did you experience today?

_____

_____

_____

_____

_____

_____

_____

_____

_____

_____

_____

_____

_____

_____

_____

_____

_____

_____

Sunshine Loves You!

Write It Out & Meditate...

Deuteronomy 4:31

_____
_____
_____
_____
_____

Talk to God...

_____
_____
_____
_____
_____
_____
_____
_____
_____
_____
_____

God loves you MORE!

What "SUNSHINE" did you experience today?

_____

_____

_____

_____

_____

_____

_____

_____

_____

_____

_____

_____

_____

_____

_____

_____

_____

_____

Sunshine Loves You!

Write It Out & Meditate...

Jeremiah 31:3

_____

_____

_____

_____

_____

Talk to God...

_____

_____

_____

_____

_____

_____

_____

_____

_____

_____

God loves you MORE!

What "SUNSHINE" did you experience today?

_____

_____

_____

_____

_____

_____

_____

_____

_____

_____

_____

_____

_____

_____

_____

_____

_____

_____

_____

Sunshine Loves You!

July 26, 2021

Write It Out & Meditate...

Matthew 5:12

_____
_____
_____
_____
_____

Talk to God...

_____
_____
_____
_____
_____
_____
_____
_____
_____
_____

God loves you MORE!

What "SUNSHINE" did you experience today?

_____

_____

_____

_____

_____

_____

_____

_____

_____

_____

_____

_____

_____

_____

_____

_____

_____

_____

_____

_____

Sunshine Loves You!

Write It Out & Meditate...

Jeremiah 32:40

_____

_____

_____

_____

_____

Talk to God...

_____

_____

_____

_____

_____

_____

_____

_____

_____

_____

_____

God loves you MORE!

What "SUNSHINE" did you experience today?

_____

_____

_____

_____

_____

_____

_____

_____

_____

_____

_____

_____

_____

_____

_____

_____

_____

_____

_____

Sunshine Loves You!

Write It Out & Meditate...

Psalm 100:5

_____

_____

_____

_____

_____

Talk to God...

_____

_____

_____

_____

_____

_____

_____

_____

_____

_____

_____

God loves you MORE!

What "SUNSHINE" did you experience today?

_____

_____

_____

_____

_____

_____

_____

_____

_____

_____

_____

_____

_____

_____

_____

_____

_____

_____

_____

Sunshine Loves You!

Write It Out & Meditate...

Hebrews 4:16

_____
_____
_____
_____
_____

Talk to God...

_____
_____
_____
_____
_____
_____
_____
_____
_____
_____
_____

God loves you MORE!

What "SUNSHINE" did you experience today?

_____

_____

_____

_____

_____

_____

_____

_____

_____

_____

_____

_____

_____

_____

_____

_____

_____

_____

_____

Sunshine Loves You!

July 30, 2021

Write It Out & Meditate...

2nd Samuel 7:28

_____
_____
_____
_____
_____

Talk to God...

_____
_____
_____
_____
_____
_____
_____
_____
_____
_____
_____
_____

God loves you MORE!

What "SUNSHINE" did you experience today?

_____
_____
_____
_____
_____
_____
_____
_____
_____
_____
_____
_____
_____
_____
_____
_____
_____
_____
_____
_____
_____

Sunshine Loves You!

July 31, 2021

Write It Out & Meditate...

Psalm 46:10

_____

_____

_____

_____

_____

Talk to God...

_____

_____

_____

_____

_____

_____

_____

_____

_____

_____

_____

God loves you MORE!

What "SUNSHINE" did you experience today?

_____

_____

_____

_____

_____

_____

_____

_____

_____

_____

_____

_____

_____

_____

_____

_____

_____

_____

_____

Sunshine Loves You!

August's

Scripture Focus

Therefore, if anyone is in Christ, he is a new creation; old things have passed away; behold, all things have become new.

2 Corinthians 5:17 NKJV

My thoughts about this Scripture:

_____

_____

_____

_____

_____

_____

_____

_____

_____

God loves you MORE!

Sunshine Loves You!

August's
Reflection & Prayer

This is a GREAT MONTH to forgive yourself, let go of your past and stop allowing your past to dictate your future. What has been done, has been done. Your mistakes do not define who you are in Christ today. There's no undoing your past; however, you have an entire new life before you to live out. Walk in the newness of life God gives you daily. Walk upright and boldly knowing that once you have sincerely repented, God has forgotten about your past, so should you. Your past was necessary for you to get to your future. Understand that what you went through was for someone you will encounter on this journey of Life. Don't ever be ashamed of your testimony. God needed YOU to go through what you went through to help encourage someone who is going to encounter the same cross you had to bear. Forgive yourself. Let go of your past. Walk in the newness of life. Encourage someone with your testimony.

Father, I thank you that you are such a loving and merciful God. Right now, I repent of all sins I have committed by both commission and omission. I repent of the sins that I may have committed that I am unaware of as well. I thank you for a fresh start. I thank you that you don't hold my sins against me; yet, you chastise me when I do wrong because you love me. You have given me the opportunity to live a new life and today I receive that new life. Help me to put on my blinders and may I only look back for a brief moment simply to see how far you have brought me from. Thank you in advance for giving me the boldness to share my testimony to encourage others on their journey.

In Jesus' Name,

AMEN.

God loves you MORE!

August 2021 (United States)

September 2021
S	M	T	W	T	F	S
			1	2	3	4
5	6	7	8	9	10	11
12	13	14	15	16	17	18
19	20	21	22	23	24	25
26	27	28	29	30		

Sun	Mon	Tue	Wed	Thu	Fri	Sat
1	2	3	4	5	6	7
8 ● New Moon	9	10	11	12	13	14
15 ◐ 1st Quarter	16	17	18	19	20	21
22 ○ Full Moon	23	24	25	26	27	28
29	30 ◑ 3rd Quarter	31	1	2	3	4

Sunshine Loves You!

Write It Out & Meditate...

John 14:6

_____

_____

_____

_____

_____

Talk to God...

_____

_____

_____

_____

_____

_____

_____

_____

_____

_____

_____

_____

God loves you MORE!

What "SUNSHINE" did you experience today?

_____

_____

_____

_____

_____

_____

_____

_____

_____

_____

_____

_____

_____

_____

_____

_____

_____

_____

_____

_____

Sunshine Loves You!

Write It Out & Meditate...

Psalm 34:8

_____

_____

_____

_____

_____

Talk to God...

_____

_____

_____

_____

_____

_____

_____

_____

_____

_____

_____

God loves you MORE!

What "SUNSHINE" did you experience today?

_____

_____

_____

_____

_____

_____

_____

_____

_____

_____

_____

_____

_____

_____

_____

_____

_____

_____

_____

_____

Sunshine Loves You!

Write It Out & Meditate...

Hebrews 9:28

_____

_____

_____

_____

_____

Talk to God...

_____

_____

_____

_____

_____

_____

_____

_____

_____

_____

_____

God loves you MORE!

What "SUNSHINE" did you experience today?

_____

_____

_____

_____

_____

_____

_____

_____

_____

_____

_____

_____

_____

_____

_____

_____

_____

_____

_____

_____

_____

Sunshine Loves You!

Write It Out & Meditate...

Matthew 5:11

_____

_____

_____

_____

_____

Talk to God...

_____

_____

_____

_____

_____

_____

_____

_____

_____

_____

_____

_____

God loves you MORE!

What "SUNSHINE" did you experience today?

_____

_____

_____

_____

_____

_____

_____

_____

_____

_____

_____

_____

_____

_____

_____

_____

_____

_____

_____

_____

_____

_____

Sunshine Loves You!

Write It Out & Meditate...

Psalm 34:10

_____
_____
_____
_____
_____

Talk to God...

_____
_____
_____
_____
_____
_____
_____
_____
_____
_____
_____

God loves you MORE!

What "SUNSHINE" did you experience today?

_____

_____

_____

_____

_____

_____

_____

_____

_____

_____

_____

_____

_____

_____

_____

_____

_____

_____

Sunshine Loves You!

Write It Out & Meditate...

John 8:12

_____
_____
_____
_____
_____

Talk to God...

_____
_____
_____
_____
_____
_____
_____
_____
_____
_____
_____

God loves you MORE!

What "SUNSHINE" did you experience today?

_____

_____

_____

_____

_____

_____

_____

_____

_____

_____

_____

_____

_____

_____

_____

_____

_____

_____

_____

_____

_____

_____

Sunshine Loves You!

August 7, 2021

Write It Out & Meditate...

Matthew 28:19-20

_____
_____
_____
_____
_____

Talk to God...

_____
_____
_____
_____
_____
_____
_____
_____
_____
_____
_____

God loves you MORE!

What "SUNSHINE" did you experience today?

_____

_____

_____

_____

_____

_____

_____

_____

_____

_____

_____

_____

_____

_____

_____

_____

_____

_____

_____

_____

Sunshine Loves You!

Write It Out & Meditate...

John 14:15

_____
_____
_____
_____
_____

Talk to God...

_____
_____
_____
_____
_____
_____
_____
_____
_____
_____
_____

God loves you MORE!

What "SUNSHINE" did you experience today?

_____

_____

_____

_____

_____

_____

_____

_____

_____

_____

_____

_____

_____

_____

_____

_____

_____

_____

_____

_____

_____

_____

Sunshine Loves You!

Write It Out & Meditate...

Jeremiah 29:12

_____

_____

_____

_____

_____

Talk to God...

_____

_____

_____

_____

_____

_____

_____

_____

_____

_____

_____

_____

God loves you MORE!

What "SUNSHINE" did you experience today?

_____
_____
_____
_____
_____
_____
_____
_____
_____
_____
_____
_____
_____
_____
_____
_____
_____
_____
_____
_____
_____
_____

Sunshine Loves You!

Write It Out & Meditate...

John 14:27

_____
_____
_____
_____
_____

Talk to God...

_____
_____
_____
_____
_____
_____
_____
_____
_____
_____
_____

God loves you MORE!

What "SUNSHINE" did you experience today?

_____

_____

_____

_____

_____

_____

_____

_____

_____

_____

_____

_____

_____

_____

_____

_____

_____

_____

_____

_____

Sunshine Loves You!

Write It Out & Meditate...

Psalm 102:17

_____

_____

_____

_____

_____

Talk to God...

_____

_____

_____

_____

_____

_____

_____

_____

_____

_____

_____

_____

God loves you MORE!

What "SUNSHINE" did you experience today?

_____
_____
_____
_____
_____
_____
_____
_____
_____
_____
_____
_____
_____
_____
_____
_____
_____
_____
_____
_____

Sunshine Loves You!

Write It Out & Meditate...

Matthew 6:33

_____
_____
_____
_____
_____

Talk to God...

_____
_____
_____
_____
_____
_____
_____
_____
_____
_____
_____

God loves you MORE!

What "SUNSHINE" did you experience today?

_____

_____

_____

_____

_____

_____

_____

_____

_____

_____

_____

_____

_____

_____

_____

_____

_____

_____

Sunshine Loves You!

Write It Out & Meditate...

John 10:10

_____
_____
_____
_____
_____

Talk to God...

_____
_____
_____
_____
_____
_____
_____
_____
_____
_____
_____
_____

God loves you MORE!

What "SUNSHINE" did you experience today?

_____

_____

_____

_____

_____

_____

_____

_____

_____

_____

_____

_____

_____

_____

_____

_____

_____

_____

_____

Sunshine Loves You!

August 14, 2021

Write It Out & Meditate...

Hebrews 4:12

_____
_____
_____
_____
_____

Talk to God...

_____
_____
_____
_____
_____
_____
_____
_____
_____
_____
_____

God loves you MORE!

What "SUNSHINE" did you experience today?

_____

_____

_____

_____

_____

_____

_____

_____

_____

_____

_____

_____

_____

_____

_____

_____

_____

_____

_____

_____

Sunshine Loves You!

August 15, 2021

Write It Out & Meditate...

2nd Corinthians 1:20

_____
_____
_____
_____
_____

Talk to God...

_____
_____
_____
_____
_____
_____
_____
_____
_____
_____

God loves you MORE!

What "SUNSHINE" did you experience today?

_____

_____

_____

_____

_____

_____

_____

_____

_____

_____

_____

_____

_____

_____

_____

_____

_____

_____

_____

_____

_____

Sunshine Loves You!

August 16, 2021

Write It Out & Meditate...

1st John 2:25

_____
_____
_____
_____
_____

Talk to God...

_____
_____
_____
_____
_____
_____
_____
_____
_____
_____
_____

God loves you MORE!

What "SUNSHINE" did you experience today?

_____

_____

_____

_____

_____

_____

_____

_____

_____

_____

_____

_____

_____

_____

_____

_____

_____

_____

_____

_____

_____

Sunshine Loves You!

Write It Out & Meditate...

2nd Corinthians 10:4-5

_____

_____

_____

_____

_____

Talk to God...

_____

_____

_____

_____

_____

_____

_____

_____

_____

_____

_____

God loves you MORE!

What "SUNSHINE" did you experience today?

_____

_____

_____

_____

_____

_____

_____

_____

_____

_____

_____

_____

_____

_____

_____

_____

_____

_____

_____

Sunshine Loves You!

August 18, 2021

Write It Out & Meditate...

Luke 18:27

_____
_____
_____
_____
_____

Talk to God...

_____
_____
_____
_____
_____
_____
_____
_____
_____
_____
_____

God loves you MORE!

What "SUNSHINE" did you experience today?

_____

_____

_____

_____

_____

_____

_____

_____

_____

_____

_____

_____

_____

_____

_____

_____

_____

_____

_____

_____

Sunshine Loves You!

Write It Out & Meditate...

Psalm 103:12

_____

_____

_____

_____

_____

Talk to God...

_____

_____

_____

_____

_____

_____

_____

_____

_____

_____

_____

God loves you MORE!

What "SUNSHINE" did you experience today?

_____

_____

_____

_____

_____

_____

_____

_____

_____

_____

_____

_____

_____

_____

_____

_____

_____

_____

_____

_____

_____

Sunshine Loves You!

August 20, 2021

Write It Out & Meditate...

Galatians 5:22-23

_____
_____
_____
_____
_____

Talk to God...

_____
_____
_____
_____
_____
_____
_____
_____
_____
_____
_____

God loves you MORE!

What "SUNSHINE" did you experience today?

_____

_____

_____

_____

_____

_____

_____

_____

_____

_____

_____

_____

_____

_____

_____

_____

_____

_____

_____

_____

Sunshine Loves You!

August 21, 2021

Write It Out & Meditate...

Galatians 5:22-23

_____
_____
_____
_____
_____

Talk to God...

_____
_____
_____
_____
_____
_____
_____
_____
_____
_____
_____

God loves you MORE!

What "SUNSHINE" did you experience today?

_____

_____

_____

_____

_____

_____

_____

_____

_____

_____

_____

_____

_____

_____

_____

_____

_____

_____

_____

_____

_____

Sunshine Loves You!

August 22, 2021

Write It Out & Meditate...

Job 13:15

_____
_____
_____
_____
_____

Talk to God...

_____
_____
_____
_____
_____
_____
_____
_____
_____
_____
_____
_____

God loves you MORE!

What "SUNSHINE" did you experience today?

_____

_____

_____

_____

_____

_____

_____

_____

_____

_____

_____

_____

_____

_____

_____

_____

_____

_____

_____

_____

_____

Sunshine Loves You!

Write It Out & Meditate...

Psalm 34:9

_____

_____

_____

_____

_____

Talk to God...

_____

_____

_____

_____

_____

_____

_____

_____

_____

_____

_____

God loves you MORE!

What "SUNSHINE" did you experience today?

_____

_____

_____

_____

_____

_____

_____

_____

_____

_____

_____

_____

_____

_____

_____

_____

_____

_____

_____

_____

Sunshine Loves You!

August 24, 2021

Write It Out & Meditate...

Joshua 1:8

_____
_____
_____
_____
_____

Talk to God...

_____
_____
_____
_____
_____
_____
_____
_____
_____
_____
_____

God loves you MORE!

What "SUNSHINE" did you experience today?

_____

_____

_____

_____

_____

_____

_____

_____

_____

_____

_____

_____

_____

_____

_____

_____

_____

_____

_____

_____

Sunshine Loves You!

Write It Out & Meditate...

2nd Corinthians 9:10

_____

_____

_____

_____

_____

Talk to God...

_____

_____

_____

_____

_____

_____

_____

_____

_____

_____

_____

God loves you MORE!

What "SUNSHINE" did you experience today?

_____

_____

_____

_____

_____

_____

_____

_____

_____

_____

_____

_____

_____

_____

_____

_____

_____

_____

Sunshine Loves You!

August 26, 2021

Write It Out & Meditate...

Exodus 15:26

_____
_____
_____
_____
_____

Talk to God...

_____
_____
_____
_____
_____
_____
_____
_____
_____
_____
_____

God loves you MORE!

What "SUNSHINE" did you experience today?

_____

_____

_____

_____

_____

_____

_____

_____

_____

_____

_____

_____

_____

_____

_____

_____

_____

_____

_____

_____

Sunshine Loves You!

Write It Out & Meditate...

John 14:1-3

_____

_____

_____

_____

_____

Talk to God...

_____

_____

_____

_____

_____

_____

_____

_____

_____

_____

_____

God loves you MORE!

What "SUNSHINE" did you experience today?

_____

_____

_____

_____

_____

_____

_____

_____

_____

_____

_____

_____

_____

_____

_____

_____

_____

_____

_____

_____

Sunshine Loves You!

August 28, 2021

Write It Out & Meditate...

Romans 13:5

_____
_____
_____
_____
_____

Talk to God...

_____
_____
_____
_____
_____
_____
_____
_____
_____
_____
_____
_____

God loves you MORE!

What "SUNSHINE" did you experience today?

_____

_____

_____

_____

_____

_____

_____

_____

_____

_____

_____

_____

_____

_____

_____

_____

_____

_____

_____

Sunshine Loves You!

August 29, 2021

Write It Out & Meditate...

2nd Timothy 4:8

_____
_____
_____
_____
_____

Talk to God...

_____
_____
_____
_____
_____
_____
_____
_____
_____
_____
_____

God loves you MORE!

What "SUNSHINE" did you experience today?

_____

_____

_____

_____

_____

_____

_____

_____

_____

_____

_____

_____

_____

_____

_____

_____

_____

_____

_____

_____

_____

_____

Sunshine Loves You!

Write It Out & Meditate...

Proverbs 18:10

_____

_____

_____

_____

_____

Talk to God...

_____

_____

_____

_____

_____

_____

_____

_____

_____

_____

God loves you MORE!

What "SUNSHINE" did you experience today?

_____

_____

_____

_____

_____

_____

_____

_____

_____

_____

_____

_____

_____

_____

_____

_____

_____

_____

_____

_____

_____

Sunshine Loves You!

Write It Out & Meditate...

Psalm 138:7

_____

_____

_____

_____

_____

Talk to God...

_____

_____

_____

_____

_____

_____

_____

_____

_____

_____

_____

God loves you MORE!

What "SUNSHINE" did you experience today?

_____

_____

_____

_____

_____

_____

_____

_____

_____

_____

_____

_____

_____

_____

_____

_____

_____

_____

Sunshine Loves You!

September's
Scripture Focus

"Therefore I tell you, whatever you ask for in prayer, believe that you have received it, and it will be yours."

Mark 11:24 NIV

My thoughts about this Scripture:

_____

_____

_____

_____

_____

_____

_____

_____

God loves you MORE!

Sunshine Loves You!

September's Reflection & Prayer

This is a GREAT MONTH to recognize the power of prayer. Often times, we naturally tend to share with others our pains, concerns and problems. And sometimes, these individuals are able to help us, but often times, they are not. However, our Father, who knows all and sees all is always able to help us. God knew you before he placed you in your mother's womb and He already knows your transition date. Certainly, if He knew you before you were born and knows when you're going to transition, He indeed knows all of the good things and challenging things that are going to happen to you between your birth and death. We are talking about a God who knows the very number of hairs that are on your head. God wants you to bring your cares (and celebrations) to Him and talk with Him about what's going on in your life. Remember, we don't serve a God who is into fancy words or eloquent prayers. God simply wants to hear from you and not just when you need Him. God is into individuals with a childlike faith, true worshippers and persons with a broken heart and a contrite spirit. Don't wait any longer. He's right there waiting to hear from you.

Father, I thank you for being a very-present God. You are a God that desires to hear from me and I have not always taken advantage of the privilege of prayer. Please forgive me for sharing my concerns with family, co-workers, strangers and not coming directly to You. Help me Father as I continue to strengthen my prayer life, that I would not just talk to you, but that I would listen to you and immediately take heed to what you're telling me to do or not to do. Thank you for allowing me to come to you with simple words. Thank you for hearing my prayers through my tears. Thank you for even hearing the unspoken prayers that rest upon my heart. You are an amazing and loving God and I thank you for building and strengthening my new prayer life.

In Jesus' Name,

AMEN.

God loves you MORE!

September 2021 (United States)

October 2021

S	M	T	W	T	F	S
					1	2
3	4	5	6	7	8	9
10	11	12	13	14	15	16
17	18	19	20	21	22	23
24	25	26	27	28	29	30
31						

Sun	Mon	Tue	Wed	Thu	Fri	Sat
29	30 ☽ 3rd Quarter	31	1	2	3	4
5	6 ● New Moon ● Labor Day	7	8	9	10	11
12	13 ☽ 1st Quarter	14	15	16	17	18
19	20 ○ Full Moon	21	22	23	24	25
26	27	28 ☽ 3rd Quarter	29	30	1	2

● Federal Holidays   ● Local Holidays   ❶ Multiple Events

Sunshine Loves You!

Write It Out & Meditate...

Micah 7:19

_____

_____

_____

_____

_____

Talk to God...

_____

_____

_____

_____

_____

_____

_____

_____

_____

_____

_____

God loves you MORE!

What "SUNSHINE" did you experience today?

_____

_____

_____

_____

_____

_____

_____

_____

_____

_____

_____

_____

_____

_____

_____

_____

_____

_____

_____

Sunshine Loves You!

Write It Out & Meditate...

Psalm 34:4

_____

_____

_____

_____

_____

Talk to God...

_____

_____

_____

_____

_____

_____

_____

_____

_____

_____

_____

God loves you MORE!

What "SUNSHINE" did you experience today?

_____

_____

_____

_____

_____

_____

_____

_____

_____

_____

_____

_____

_____

_____

_____

_____

_____

_____

_____

Sunshine Loves You!

September 3, 2021

Write It Out & Meditate...

Romans 8:37

_____

_____

_____

_____

_____

Talk to God...

_____

_____

_____

_____

_____

_____

_____

_____

_____

_____

God loves you MORE!

What "SUNSHINE" did you experience today?

_____

_____

_____

_____

_____

_____

_____

_____

_____

_____

_____

_____

_____

_____

_____

_____

_____

_____

_____

Sunshine Loves You!

Write It Out & Meditate...

1st John 4:18

_____

_____

_____

_____

_____

Talk to God...

_____

_____

_____

_____

_____

_____

_____

_____

_____

_____

_____

God loves you MORE!

What "SUNSHINE" did you experience today?

_____

_____

_____

_____

_____

_____

_____

_____

_____

_____

_____

_____

_____

_____

_____

_____

_____

_____

_____

_____

Sunshine Loves You!

September 5, 2021

Write It Out & Meditate...

Psalm 139:13

_____

_____

_____

_____

_____

Talk to God...

_____

_____

_____

_____

_____

_____

_____

_____

_____

_____

God loves you MORE!

What "SUNSHINE" did you experience today?

_____

_____

_____

_____

_____

_____

_____

_____

_____

_____

_____

_____

_____

_____

_____

_____

_____

_____

_____

Sunshine Loves You!

Write It Out & Meditate...

Ephesians 6:14-17

_____
_____
_____
_____
_____

Talk to God...

_____
_____
_____
_____
_____
_____
_____
_____
_____
_____
_____

God loves you MORE!

What "SUNSHINE" did you experience today?

_____

_____

_____

_____

_____

_____

_____

_____

_____

_____

_____

_____

_____

_____

_____

_____

_____

_____

_____

Sunshine Loves You!

Write It Out & Meditate...

2nd Corinthians 4:18

_____

_____

_____

_____

_____

Talk to God...

_____

_____

_____

_____

_____

_____

_____

_____

_____

_____

_____

God loves you MORE!

What "SUNSHINE" did you experience today?

_____

_____

_____

_____

_____

_____

_____

_____

_____

_____

_____

_____

_____

_____

_____

_____

_____

_____

_____

Sunshine Loves You!

Write It Out & Meditate...

Isaiah 43:1

_____

_____

_____

_____

_____

Talk to God...

_____

_____

_____

_____

_____

_____

_____

_____

_____

_____

_____

God loves you MORE!

What "SUNSHINE" did you experience today?

_____

_____

_____

_____

_____

_____

_____

_____

_____

_____

_____

_____

_____

_____

_____

_____

_____

_____

Sunshine Loves You!

September 9, 2021

Write It Out & Meditate...

Psalm 5:12

_____
_____
_____
_____
_____

Talk to God...

_____
_____
_____
_____
_____
_____
_____
_____
_____
_____
_____

God loves you MORE!

What "SUNSHINE" did you experience today?

_____

_____

_____

_____

_____

_____

_____

_____

_____

_____

_____

_____

_____

_____

_____

_____

_____

_____

_____

Sunshine Loves You!

Write It Out & Meditate...

Matthew 5:4

_____

_____

_____

_____

_____

Talk to God...

_____

_____

_____

_____

_____

_____

_____

_____

_____

_____

_____

God loves you MORE!

What "SUNSHINE" did you experience today?

_____

_____

_____

_____

_____

_____

_____

_____

_____

_____

_____

_____

_____

_____

_____

_____

_____

_____

Sunshine Loves You!

Write It Out & Meditate...

Psalm 121:5-6

_____

_____

_____

_____

_____

Talk to God...

_____

_____

_____

_____

_____

_____

_____

_____

_____

_____

_____

_____

God loves you MORE!

What "SUNSHINE" did you experience today?

_____

_____

_____

_____

_____

_____

_____

_____

_____

_____

_____

_____

_____

_____

_____

_____

_____

_____

_____

Sunshine Loves You!

Write It Out & Meditate...

Matthew 5:14-16

_____

_____

_____

_____

_____

Talk to God...

_____

_____

_____

_____

_____

_____

_____

_____

_____

_____

_____

God loves you MORE!

What "SUNSHINE" did you experience today?

_____

_____

_____

_____

_____

_____

_____

_____

_____

_____

_____

_____

_____

_____

_____

_____

_____

_____

Sunshine Loves You!

Write It Out & Meditate...

Ephesians 3:20-21

_____

_____

_____

_____

_____

Talk to God...

_____

_____

_____

_____

_____

_____

_____

_____

_____

_____

_____

God loves you MORE!

What "SUNSHINE" did you experience today?

_____

_____

_____

_____

_____

_____

_____

_____

_____

_____

_____

_____

_____

_____

_____

_____

_____

_____

Sunshine Loves You!

Write It Out & Meditate...

2nd Corinthians 9:11

_____

_____

_____

_____

_____

Talk to God...

_____

_____

_____

_____

_____

_____

_____

_____

_____

_____

_____

God loves you MORE!

What "SUNSHINE" did you experience today?

_____

_____

_____

_____

_____

_____

_____

_____

_____

_____

_____

_____

_____

_____

_____

_____

_____

_____

_____

_____

_____

Sunshine Loves You!

Write It Out & Meditate...

1st Peter 3:11-12

_____

_____

_____

_____

_____

Talk to God...

_____

_____

_____

_____

_____

_____

_____

_____

_____

_____

_____

God loves you MORE!

What "SUNSHINE" did you experience today?

_____

_____

_____

_____

_____

_____

_____

_____

_____

_____

_____

_____

_____

_____

_____

_____

_____

_____

_____

_____

Sunshine Loves You!

September 16, 2021

Write It Out & Meditate...

Psalm 91:5-6

_____
_____
_____
_____
_____

Talk to God...

_____
_____
_____
_____
_____
_____
_____
_____
_____
_____
_____

God loves you MORE!

What "SUNSHINE" did you experience today?

_____

_____

_____

_____

_____

_____

_____

_____

_____

_____

_____

_____

_____

_____

_____

_____

_____

_____

_____

_____

Sunshine Loves You!

September 17, 2021

Write It Out & Meditate...

Matthew 19:14

_____
_____
_____
_____
_____

Talk to God...

_____
_____
_____
_____
_____
_____
_____
_____
_____
_____
_____

God loves you MORE!

What "SUNSHINE" did you experience today?

_____

_____

_____

_____

_____

_____

_____

_____

_____

_____

_____

_____

_____

_____

_____

_____

_____

_____

_____

_____

Sunshine Loves You!

September 18, 2021

Write It Out & Meditate...

Proverbs 13:4

_____
_____
_____
_____
_____

Talk to God...

_____
_____
_____
_____
_____
_____
_____
_____
_____
_____
_____

God loves you MORE!

What "SUNSHINE" did you experience today?

_____

_____

_____

_____

_____

_____

_____

_____

_____

_____

_____

_____

_____

_____

_____

_____

_____

_____

_____

_____

_____

Sunshine Loves You!

September 19, 2021

Write It Out & Meditate...

Psalm 46:1

_____

_____

_____

_____

_____

Talk to God...

_____

_____

_____

_____

_____

_____

_____

_____

_____

_____

_____

God loves you MORE!

What "SUNSHINE" did you experience today?

_____

_____

_____

_____

_____

_____

_____

_____

_____

_____

_____

_____

_____

_____

_____

_____

_____

_____

_____

_____

Sunshine Loves You!

Write It Out & Meditate...

1st Corinthians 9:25

_____

_____

_____

_____

_____

Talk to God...

_____

_____

_____

_____

_____

_____

_____

_____

_____

_____

_____

God loves you MORE!

What "SUNSHINE" did you experience today?

_____

_____

_____

_____

_____

_____

_____

_____

_____

_____

_____

_____

_____

_____

_____

_____

_____

_____

_____

_____

Sunshine Loves You!

Write It Out & Meditate...

Romans 12:21

_____

_____

_____

_____

_____

Talk to God...

_____

_____

_____

_____

_____

_____

_____

_____

_____

_____

God loves you MORE!

What "SUNSHINE" did you experience today?

_____

_____

_____

_____

_____

_____

_____

_____

_____

_____

_____

_____

_____

_____

_____

_____

_____

_____

_____

_____

_____

Sunshine Loves You!

September 22, 2021

Write It Out & Meditate...

Matthew 7:7

_____
_____
_____
_____
_____

Talk to God...

_____
_____
_____
_____
_____
_____
_____
_____
_____
_____
_____
_____

God loves you MORE!

What "SUNSHINE" did you experience today?

_____

_____

_____

_____

_____

_____

_____

_____

_____

_____

_____

_____

_____

_____

_____

_____

_____

_____

_____

_____

Sunshine Loves You!

Write It Out & Meditate...

Philippians 2:12-13

_____

_____

_____

_____

_____

Talk to God...

_____

_____

_____

_____

_____

_____

_____

_____

_____

_____

_____

_____

God loves you MORE!

What "SUNSHINE" did you experience today?

_____

_____

_____

_____

_____

_____

_____

_____

_____

_____

_____

_____

_____

_____

_____

_____

_____

_____

_____

_____

Sunshine Loves You!

September 24, 2021

Write It Out & Meditate...

Colossians 1:9-10

_____

_____

_____

_____

_____

Talk to God...

_____

_____

_____

_____

_____

_____

_____

_____

_____

_____

_____

God loves you MORE!

What "SUNSHINE" did you experience today?

_____
_____
_____
_____
_____
_____
_____
_____
_____
_____
_____
_____
_____
_____
_____
_____
_____
_____
_____

Sunshine Loves You!

Write It Out & Meditate...

2nd Timothy 2:15

_____
_____
_____
_____
_____

Talk to God...

_____
_____
_____
_____
_____
_____
_____
_____
_____
_____
_____

God loves you MORE!

What "SUNSHINE" did you experience today?

_____

_____

_____

_____

_____

_____

_____

_____

_____

_____

_____

_____

_____

_____

_____

_____

_____

_____

_____

_____

Sunshine Loves You!

Write It Out & Meditate...

Proverbs 16:17

_____

_____

_____

_____

_____

Talk to God...

_____

_____

_____

_____

_____

_____

_____

_____

_____

_____

_____

_____

God loves you MORE!

What "SUNSHINE" did you experience today?

_____

_____

_____

_____

_____

_____

_____

_____

_____

_____

_____

_____

_____

_____

_____

_____

_____

_____

_____

_____

Sunshine Loves You!

Write It Out & Meditate...

Psalm 41:1

_____
_____
_____
_____
_____

Talk to God...

_____
_____
_____
_____
_____
_____
_____
_____
_____
_____
_____
_____
_____

God loves you MORE!

What "SUNSHINE" did you experience today?

_____

_____

_____

_____

_____

_____

_____

_____

_____

_____

_____

_____

_____

_____

_____

_____

_____

_____

_____

_____

Sunshine Loves You!

Write It Out & Meditate...

Romans 8:5

_____

_____

_____

_____

_____

Talk to God...

_____

_____

_____

_____

_____

_____

_____

_____

_____

_____

_____

God loves you MORE!

What "SUNSHINE" did you experience today?

_____

_____

_____

_____

_____

_____

_____

_____

_____

_____

_____

_____

_____

_____

_____

_____

_____

_____

_____

_____

Sunshine Loves You!

September 29, 2021

Write It Out & Meditate...

Titus 2:11-12

_____
_____
_____
_____
_____

Talk to God...

_____
_____
_____
_____
_____
_____
_____
_____
_____
_____
_____
_____

God loves you MORE!

What "SUNSHINE" did you experience today?

_____

_____

_____

_____

_____

_____

_____

_____

_____

_____

_____

_____

_____

_____

_____

_____

_____

_____

_____

_____

Sunshine Loves You!

September 30, 2021

Write It Out & Meditate...

Matthew 6:34

_____

_____

_____

_____

_____

Talk to God...

_____

_____

_____

_____

_____

_____

_____

_____

_____

_____

_____

God loves you MORE!

What "SUNSHINE" did you experience today?

_____

_____

_____

_____

_____

_____

_____

_____

_____

_____

_____

_____

_____

_____

_____

_____

_____

_____

_____

_____

_____

Sunshine Loves You!

October's

Scripture Focus

Death and life are in

the power of the tongue.

Proverbs 18:21 NASB

My thoughts about this Scripture:

_____

_____

_____

_____

_____

_____

_____

_____

_____

God loves you MORE!

Sunshine Loves You!

October's Reflection & Prayer

Today is a GREAT MONTH to be careful as to what comes out of your mouth about yourself and others. Replace all of your negative thoughts and speech about yourself and others with positive affirmations. Consider softening your words with people even when correction may be needed. Encourage, comfort and console those with whom you encounter this month. Let them leave your presence feeling God's love. Warm the lives of others around you by displaying a Christlike attitude. Remember, someone needs your tongue to positively speak into their life to get them through their hurt, pain or sorrow. But also remember, you have that same power to speak positively into your own life to help you get through your hurt, pain and sorrow. Don't give up the fight. Speak life.

Father, I thank you for being an awesome God and teaching me how to use my tongue to edify, encourage and enlighten. I repent for using this small, yet powerful tool in a manner sometimes that wasn't pleasing to you. Forgive me for using my tongue to tear down myself and others. Help me to consider my words before they depart from my lips, understanding that my tongue has the ability to give life to a situation or absolutely destroy a situation. Help me to use my tongue to begin to move mountains in my life. Help me to use my tongue to speak forth those things that are yet to be.

In Jesus' Name,
AMEN.

God loves you MORE!

October 2021 (United States)

November 2021

S	M	T	W	T	F	S
	1	2	3	4	5	6
7	8	9	10	11	12	13
14	15	16	17	18	19	20
21	22	23	24	25	26	27
28	29	30				

Sun	Mon	Tue	Wed	Thu	Fri	Sat
26	27	28 ☽ First Quarter	29	30	1	2
3	4	5	6 ● New Moon	7	8	9
10	11 ● Columbus Day	12 ☽ 1st Quarter	13	14	15	16
17	18	19	20 ○ Full Moon	21	22	23
24	25	26	27	28 ☽ 3rd Quarter	29	30
31 Halloween	1	2 Daylight Sav...	3	4 ● New Moon	5	6

● Federal Holidays ● Local Holidays ☽ Moon Phase Events

Sunshine Loves You!

October 1, 2021

Write It Out & Meditate...

James 5:11

_____

_____

_____

_____

_____

Talk to God...

_____

_____

_____

_____

_____

_____

_____

_____

_____

_____

_____

God loves you MORE!

What "SUNSHINE" did you experience today?

_____
_____
_____
_____
_____
_____
_____
_____
_____
_____
_____
_____
_____
_____
_____
_____
_____
_____
_____

Sunshine Loves You!

Write It Out & Meditate...

Romans 13:14

_____

_____

_____

_____

_____

Talk to God...

_____

_____

_____

_____

_____

_____

_____

_____

_____

_____

_____

God loves you MORE!

What "SUNSHINE" did you experience today?

_____

_____

_____

_____

_____

_____

_____

_____

_____

_____

_____

_____

_____

_____

_____

_____

_____

_____

_____

_____

Sunshine Loves You!

October 3, 2021

Write It Out & Meditate...

Matthew 5:6

_____

_____

_____

_____

_____

Talk to God...

_____

_____

_____

_____

_____

_____

_____

_____

_____

_____

_____

_____

God loves you MORE!

What "SUNSHINE" did you experience today?

_____

_____

_____

_____

_____

_____

_____

_____

_____

_____

_____

_____

_____

_____

_____

_____

_____

_____

_____

_____

_____

Sunshine Loves You!

Write It Out & Meditate...

1st Corinthians 6:20

_____

_____

_____

_____

_____

Talk to God...

_____

_____

_____

_____

_____

_____

_____

_____

_____

_____

_____

God loves you MORE!

What "SUNSHINE" did you experience today?

_____

_____

_____

_____

_____

_____

_____

_____

_____

_____

_____

_____

_____

_____

_____

_____

_____

_____

_____

_____

Sunshine Loves You!

Write It Out & Meditate...

1st Timothy 4:8

_____
_____
_____
_____
_____

Talk to God...

_____
_____
_____
_____
_____
_____
_____
_____
_____
_____
_____
_____

God loves you MORE!

What "SUNSHINE" did you experience today?

_____

_____

_____

_____

_____

_____

_____

_____

_____

_____

_____

_____

_____

_____

_____

_____

_____

_____

_____

Sunshine Loves You!

Write It Out & Meditate...

Romans 12:10

_____

_____

_____

_____

_____

Talk to God...

_____

_____

_____

_____

_____

_____

_____

_____

_____

_____

_____

_____

God loves you MORE!

What "SUNSHINE" did you experience today?

_____

_____

_____

_____

_____

_____

_____

_____

_____

_____

_____

_____

_____

_____

_____

_____

_____

_____

_____

_____

Sunshine Loves You!

Write It Out & Meditate...

Psalm 4:8

_____

_____

_____

_____

_____

Talk to God...

_____

_____

_____

_____

_____

_____

_____

_____

_____

_____

_____

_____

God loves you MORE!

What "SUNSHINE" did you experience today?

_____

_____

_____

_____

_____

_____

_____

_____

_____

_____

_____

_____

_____

_____

_____

_____

_____

_____

_____

_____

_____

Sunshine Loves You!

Write It Out & Meditate...

1ˢᵗ Thessalonians 5:11

_____

_____

_____

_____

_____

Talk to God...

_____

_____

_____

_____

_____

_____

_____

_____

_____

_____

_____

God loves you MORE!

What "SUNSHINE" did you experience today?

_____

_____

_____

_____

_____

_____

_____

_____

_____

_____

_____

_____

_____

_____

_____

_____

_____

_____

_____

_____

_____

Sunshine Loves You!

Write It Out & Meditate...

Hebrews 13:1

_____
_____
_____
_____
_____

Talk to God...

_____
_____
_____
_____
_____
_____
_____
_____
_____
_____
_____

God loves you MORE!

What "SUNSHINE" did you experience today?

_____

_____

_____

_____

_____

_____

_____

_____

_____

_____

_____

_____

_____

_____

_____

_____

_____

_____

_____

_____

Sunshine Loves You!

October 10, 2021

Write It Out & Meditate...

2nd Timothy 2:16

_____
_____
_____
_____
_____

Talk to God...

_____
_____
_____
_____
_____
_____
_____
_____
_____
_____
_____
_____

God loves you MORE!

What "SUNSHINE" did you experience today?

_____

_____

_____

_____

_____

_____

_____

_____

_____

_____

_____

_____

_____

_____

_____

_____

_____

_____

_____

Sunshine Loves You!

Write It Out & Meditate...

Romans 10:11

_____

_____

_____

_____

_____

Talk to God...

_____

_____

_____

_____

_____

_____

_____

_____

_____

_____

_____

God loves you MORE!

What "SUNSHINE" did you experience today?

_____
_____
_____
_____
_____
_____
_____
_____
_____
_____
_____
_____
_____
_____
_____
_____
_____
_____
_____
_____
_____

Sunshine Loves You!

Write It Out & Meditate...

Ephesians 6:18

_____

_____

_____

_____

_____

Talk to God...

_____

_____

_____

_____

_____

_____

_____

_____

_____

_____

_____

God loves you MORE!

What "SUNSHINE" did you experience today?

_____

_____

_____

_____

_____

_____

_____

_____

_____

_____

_____

_____

_____

_____

_____

_____

_____

_____

_____

_____

Sunshine Loves You!

Write It Out & Meditate...

Psalm 37:27

_____

_____

_____

_____

_____

Talk to God...

_____

_____

_____

_____

_____

_____

_____

_____

_____

_____

_____

God loves you MORE!

What "SUNSHINE" did you experience today?

_____

_____

_____

_____

_____

_____

_____

_____

_____

_____

_____

_____

_____

_____

_____

_____

_____

_____

_____

_____

_____

Sunshine Loves You!

Write It Out & Meditate...

John 13:34

_____
_____
_____
_____
_____

Talk to God...

_____
_____
_____
_____
_____
_____
_____
_____
_____
_____
_____

God loves you MORE!

What "SUNSHINE" did you experience today?

_____

_____

_____

_____

_____

_____

_____

_____

_____

_____

_____

_____

_____

_____

_____

_____

_____

_____

_____

Sunshine Loves You!

Write It Out & Meditate...

1st Corinthians 13:13

_____

_____

_____

_____

_____

Talk to God...

_____

_____

_____

_____

_____

_____

_____

_____

_____

_____

_____

God loves you MORE!

What "SUNSHINE" did you experience today?

_____

_____

_____

_____

_____

_____

_____

_____

_____

_____

_____

_____

_____

_____

_____

_____

_____

_____

_____

_____

Sunshine Loves You!

October 16, 2021

Write It Out & Meditate...

1st John 3:18

_____
_____
_____
_____
_____

Talk to God...

_____
_____
_____
_____
_____
_____
_____
_____
_____
_____
_____

God loves you MORE!

What "SUNSHINE" did you experience today?

_____

_____

_____

_____

_____

_____

_____

_____

_____

_____

_____

_____

_____

_____

_____

_____

_____

_____

_____

Sunshine Loves You!

Write It Out & Meditate...

Romans 12:2

_____

_____

_____

_____

_____

Talk to God...

_____

_____

_____

_____

_____

_____

_____

_____

_____

_____

_____

God loves you MORE!

What "SUNSHINE" did you experience today?

_____

_____

_____

_____

_____

_____

_____

_____

_____

_____

_____

_____

_____

_____

_____

_____

_____

_____

_____

_____

_____

_____

Sunshine Loves You!

October 18, 2021

Write It Out & Meditate...

Philippians 3:13-14

_____
_____
_____
_____
_____

Talk to God...

_____
_____
_____
_____
_____
_____
_____
_____
_____
_____
_____

God loves you MORE!

What "SUNSHINE" did you experience today?

_____
_____
_____
_____
_____
_____
_____
_____
_____
_____
_____
_____
_____
_____
_____
_____
_____
_____
_____
_____
_____

Sunshine Loves You!

Write It Out & Meditate...

1st Corinthians 15:58

_____
_____
_____
_____
_____

Talk to God...

_____
_____
_____
_____
_____
_____
_____
_____
_____
_____
_____
_____

God loves you MORE!

What "SUNSHINE" did you experience today?

_____

_____

_____

_____

_____

_____

_____

_____

_____

_____

_____

_____

_____

_____

_____

_____

_____

_____

_____

Sunshine Loves You!

Write It Out & Meditate...

Luke 1:37

_____
_____
_____
_____
_____

Talk to God...

_____
_____
_____
_____
_____
_____
_____
_____
_____
_____
_____

God loves you MORE!

What "SUNSHINE" did you experience today?

_____

_____

_____

_____

_____

_____

_____

_____

_____

_____

_____

_____

_____

_____

_____

_____

_____

_____

_____

Sunshine Loves You!

October 21, 2021

Write It Out & Meditate...

1st John 4:19

_____
_____
_____
_____
_____

Talk to God...

_____
_____
_____
_____
_____
_____
_____
_____
_____
_____
_____

God loves you MORE!

What "SUNSHINE" did you experience today?

_____

_____

_____

_____

_____

_____

_____

_____

_____

_____

_____

_____

_____

_____

_____

_____

_____

_____

_____

_____

Sunshine Loves You!

Write It Out & Meditate...

Hebrews 10:23

_____

_____

_____

_____

_____

Talk to God...

_____

_____

_____

_____

_____

_____

_____

_____

_____

_____

_____

_____

God loves you MORE!

What "SUNSHINE" did you experience today?

_____

_____

_____

_____

_____

_____

_____

_____

_____

_____

_____

_____

_____

_____

_____

_____

_____

_____

_____

_____

Sunshine Loves You!

Write It Out & Meditate...

1st Peter 5:10

_____

_____

_____

_____

_____

Talk to God...

_____

_____

_____

_____

_____

_____

_____

_____

_____

_____

_____

_____

God loves you MORE!

What "SUNSHINE" did you experience today?

_____

_____

_____

_____

_____

_____

_____

_____

_____

_____

_____

_____

_____

_____

_____

_____

_____

_____

_____

_____

Sunshine Loves You!

October 24, 2021

Write It Out & Meditate...

Hebrews 13:2

_____

_____

_____

_____

_____

Talk to God...

_____

_____

_____

_____

_____

_____

_____

_____

_____

_____

_____

God loves you MORE!

What "SUNSHINE" did you experience today?

_____

_____

_____

_____

_____

_____

_____

_____

_____

_____

_____

_____

_____

_____

_____

_____

_____

_____

_____

_____

_____

Sunshine Loves You!

Write It Out & Meditate...

Romans 12:9

_____

_____

_____

_____

_____

Talk to God...

_____

_____

_____

_____

_____

_____

_____

_____

_____

_____

_____

_____

God loves you MORE!

What "SUNSHINE" did you experience today?

_____

_____

_____

_____

_____

_____

_____

_____

_____

_____

_____

_____

_____

_____

_____

_____

_____

_____

_____

Sunshine Loves You!

Write It Out & Meditate...

Psalm 91:7

_____

_____

_____

_____

_____

Talk to God...

_____

_____

_____

_____

_____

_____

_____

_____

_____

_____

_____

_____

God loves you MORE!

What "SUNSHINE" did you experience today?

_____

_____

_____

_____

_____

_____

_____

_____

_____

_____

_____

_____

_____

_____

_____

_____

_____

_____

Sunshine Loves You!

Write It Out & Meditate...

Hebrews 11:1

_____

_____

_____

_____

_____

Talk to God...

_____

_____

_____

_____

_____

_____

_____

_____

_____

_____

_____

_____

God loves you MORE!

What "SUNSHINE" did you experience today?

_____

_____

_____

_____

_____

_____

_____

_____

_____

_____

_____

_____

_____

_____

_____

_____

_____

_____

_____

_____

Sunshine Loves You!

Write It Out & Meditate...

1st Chronicles 16:11

_____

_____

_____

_____

_____

Talk to God...

_____

_____

_____

_____

_____

_____

_____

_____

_____

_____

_____

_____

God loves you MORE!

What "SUNSHINE" did you experience today?

_____

_____

_____

_____

_____

_____

_____

_____

_____

_____

_____

_____

_____

_____

_____

_____

_____

_____

Sunshine Loves You!

Write It Out & Meditate...

Matthew 5:7

_____
_____
_____
_____
_____

Talk to God...

_____
_____
_____
_____
_____
_____
_____
_____
_____
_____
_____
_____

God loves you MORE!

What "SUNSHINE" did you experience today?

_____

_____

_____

_____

_____

_____

_____

_____

_____

_____

_____

_____

_____

_____

_____

_____

_____

_____

_____

Sunshine Loves You!

Write It Out & Meditate...

1st John 4:4

_____
_____
_____
_____
_____

Talk to God...

_____
_____
_____
_____
_____
_____
_____
_____
_____
_____
_____

God loves you MORE!

What "SUNSHINE" did you experience today?

_____

_____

_____

_____

_____

_____

_____

_____

_____

_____

_____

_____

_____

_____

_____

_____

_____

_____

_____

_____

Sunshine Loves You!

Write It Out & Meditate...

1st Timothy 6:12

_____

_____

_____

_____

_____

Talk to God...

_____

_____

_____

_____

_____

_____

_____

_____

_____

_____

_____

_____

God loves you MORE!

What "SUNSHINE" did you experience today?

_____
_____
_____
_____
_____
_____
_____
_____
_____
_____
_____
_____
_____
_____
_____
_____
_____
_____
_____
_____

Sunshine Loves You!

November's
Scripture Focus

"Therefore I tell you, do not worry about your life, what you will eat or drink; or about your body, what you will wear. Is not life more than food, and the body more than clothes? Look at the birds of the air; they do not sow or reap or store away in barns, and yet your heavenly Father feeds them. Are you not much more valuable than they?"

Matthew 6:25-26 NIV

My thoughts about this Scripture:

_____

_____

_____

_____

God loves you MORE!

Sunshine Loves You!

November's Reflection & Prayer

This is a GREAT MONTH to stop worrying about everything. Make your days good, your noons better and your nights best by placing all of your concerns at His feet. God knows what you need and will supply all of your needs. Think about the last time you actually went without a need. This is probably a very difficult assignment because the reality is your God has provided you with all of your needs. God has taken care of and continues to take care of you. Stop shortchanging God. Give credit where credit is due. He is an outstanding provider, even when we have been so ungrateful at times. Look closely and see how abundantly blessed you really are. Consider giving away gently used items to someone in need. Consider sponsoring a meal for a family/person in need. Consider paying it forward at the grocery store/restaurant. We are blessed to be a blessing. Allow God's blessing to continue to flow into your life this month by being a blessing to others.

Father, I thank you for being my way maker. You are such an amazing God as you always take great care of me. As I look over my life, I have worried about things. I have worried about what people think and what they say. I have worried about situations that were beyond my control. And none of this worrying got me anywhere. I can honestly say that you have made a way when I couldn't see a way. You continue to make a way. Strengthen my Faith God to solely rely on you like the birds of the air. They don't worry; yet, they move about knowing they will be fully taken care of by you. I know the effects of worrying and understand nothing good comes from worrying. So, from this day forward, I vow to stop worrying about my life. I vow to stop worrying about what I will eat or drink. I vow to stop worrying about my body. I vow to stop worrying about what I will wear. And I vow to start trusting you more. Thank you for blessing me abundantly. Show me how I can be a blessing to others. I'm eternally thankful for all you have done for me and simply want to be a blessing to others and to give you Glory with what you have given me.

In Jesus' Name,

AMEN.

God loves you MORE!

November 2021 (United States)

December 2021
S M T W T F S
1 2 3 4
5 6 7 8 9 10 11
12 13 14 15 16 17 18
19 20 21 22 23 24 25
26 27 28 29 30 31

Sun	Mon	Tue	Wed	Thu	Fri	Sat
31 Halloween	1	2 Election Day	3	4 ● New Moon	5	6
7	8	9	10	11 ☽ 1st Quarter ● Veterans Day	12	13
14	15	16	17	18	19 ○ Full Moon	20
21	22	23	24	25 ● Thanksgiving Day	26 Black Friday	27 ☽ 3rd Quarter
28	29	30	1	2	3	4 ● New Moon

● Federal Holidays   ● Local Holidays   ●) Multiple Feph's

Sunshine Loves You!

Write It Out & Meditate...

Psalm 37:10-11

_____
_____
_____
_____
_____

Talk to God...

_____
_____
_____
_____
_____
_____
_____
_____
_____
_____
_____
_____

God loves you MORE!

What "SUNSHINE" did you experience today?

_____
_____
_____
_____
_____
_____
_____
_____
_____
_____
_____
_____
_____
_____
_____
_____
_____
_____
_____
_____
_____

Sunshine Loves You!

Write It Out & Meditate...

2nd Corinthians 5:7

_____

_____

_____

_____

_____

Talk to God...

_____

_____

_____

_____

_____

_____

_____

_____

_____

_____

_____

God loves you MORE!

What "SUNSHINE" did you experience today?

_____

_____

_____

_____

_____

_____

_____

_____

_____

_____

_____

_____

_____

_____

_____

_____

_____

_____

_____

_____

Sunshine Loves You!

Write It Out & Meditate...

Romans 12:11

_____

_____

_____

_____

_____

Talk to God...

_____

_____

_____

_____

_____

_____

_____

_____

_____

_____

_____

_____

God loves you MORE!

What "SUNSHINE" did you experience today?

_____

_____

_____

_____

_____

_____

_____

_____

_____

_____

_____

_____

_____

_____

_____

_____

_____

_____

_____

_____

_____

_____

Sunshine Loves You!

Write It Out & Meditate...

Psalm 4:3

_____
_____
_____
_____
_____

Talk to God...

_____
_____
_____
_____
_____
_____
_____
_____
_____
_____
_____

God loves you MORE!

What "SUNSHINE" did you experience today?

_____

_____

_____

_____

_____

_____

_____

_____

_____

_____

_____

_____

_____

_____

_____

_____

_____

_____

_____

_____

Sunshine Loves You!

Write It Out & Meditate...

Matthew 5:3

_____

_____

_____

_____

_____

Talk to God...

_____

_____

_____

_____

_____

_____

_____

_____

_____

_____

_____

God loves you MORE!

What "SUNSHINE" did you experience today?

_____
_____
_____
_____
_____
_____
_____
_____
_____
_____
_____
_____
_____
_____
_____
_____
_____
_____
_____
_____

Sunshine Loves You!

November 6, 2021

Write It Out & Meditate...

Psalm 73:26

_____
_____
_____
_____
_____

Talk to God...

_____
_____
_____
_____
_____
_____
_____
_____
_____
_____
_____
_____

God loves you MORE!

What "SUNSHINE" did you experience today?

_____
_____
_____
_____
_____
_____
_____
_____
_____
_____
_____
_____
_____
_____
_____
_____
_____
_____
_____
_____
_____
_____

Sunshine Loves You!

Write It Out & Meditate...

Ephesians 2:8-9

_____

_____

_____

_____

_____

Talk to God...

_____

_____

_____

_____

_____

_____

_____

_____

_____

_____

_____

_____

God loves you MORE!

What "SUNSHINE" did you experience today?

_____
_____
_____
_____
_____
_____
_____
_____
_____
_____
_____
_____
_____
_____
_____
_____
_____
_____

Sunshine Loves You!

Write It Out & Meditate...

Matthew 21:21

_____
_____
_____
_____
_____

Talk to God...

_____
_____
_____
_____
_____
_____
_____
_____
_____
_____
_____

God loves you MORE!

What "SUNSHINE" did you experience today?

_____

_____

_____

_____

_____

_____

_____

_____

_____

_____

_____

_____

_____

_____

_____

_____

_____

_____

_____

_____

Sunshine Loves You!

Write It Out & Meditate...

Romans 12:12

_____

_____

_____

_____

_____

Talk to God...

_____

_____

_____

_____

_____

_____

_____

_____

_____

_____

_____

God loves you MORE!

What "SUNSHINE" did you experience today?

_____
_____
_____
_____
_____
_____
_____
_____
_____
_____
_____
_____
_____
_____
_____
_____
_____
_____
_____
_____
_____
_____

Sunshine Loves You!

November 10, 2021

Write It Out & Meditate...

Psalm 23:5-6

_____
_____
_____
_____
_____

Talk to God...

_____
_____
_____
_____
_____
_____
_____
_____
_____
_____
_____
_____

God loves you MORE!

What "SUNSHINE" did you experience today?

_____
_____
_____
_____
_____
_____
_____
_____
_____
_____
_____
_____
_____
_____
_____
_____
_____
_____
_____
_____

Sunshine Loves You!

Write It Out & Meditate...

Hebrews 11:6

_____
_____
_____
_____
_____

Talk to God...

_____
_____
_____
_____
_____
_____
_____
_____
_____
_____
_____
_____

God loves you MORE!

What "SUNSHINE" did you experience today?

_____

_____

_____

_____

_____

_____

_____

_____

_____

_____

_____

_____

_____

_____

_____

_____

_____

_____

_____

Sunshine Loves You!

Write It Out & Meditate...

Psalm 91:4

_____

_____

_____

_____

_____

Talk to God...

_____

_____

_____

_____

_____

_____

_____

_____

_____

_____

_____

_____

God loves you MORE!

What "SUNSHINE" did you experience today?

_____

_____

_____

_____

_____

_____

_____

_____

_____

_____

_____

_____

_____

_____

_____

_____

_____

_____

_____

_____

_____

_____

Sunshine Loves You!

November 13, 2021

Write It Out & Meditate...

Matthew 5:8

_____
_____
_____
_____
_____

Talk to God...

_____
_____
_____
_____
_____
_____
_____
_____
_____
_____
_____
_____

God loves you MORE!

What "SUNSHINE" did you experience today?

_____

_____

_____

_____

_____

_____

_____

_____

_____

_____

_____

_____

_____

_____

_____

_____

_____

_____

_____

_____

Sunshine Loves You!

Write It Out & Meditate...

Psalm 30:11

_____

_____

_____

_____

_____

Talk to God...

_____

_____

_____

_____

_____

_____

_____

_____

_____

_____

_____

God loves you MORE!

What "SUNSHINE" did you experience today?

_____

_____

_____

_____

_____

_____

_____

_____

_____

_____

_____

_____

_____

_____

_____

_____

_____

_____

_____

_____

Sunshine Loves You!

Write It Out & Meditate...

Psalm 9:10

_____

_____

_____

_____

_____

Talk to God...

_____

_____

_____

_____

_____

_____

_____

_____

_____

_____

_____

_____

God loves you MORE!

What "SUNSHINE" did you experience today?

_____

_____

_____

_____

_____

_____

_____

_____

_____

_____

_____

_____

_____

_____

_____

_____

_____

_____

_____

_____

Sunshine Loves You!

Write It Out & Meditate...

Romans 12:15

_____

_____

_____

_____

_____

Talk to God...

_____

_____

_____

_____

_____

_____

_____

_____

_____

_____

_____

God loves you MORE!

What "SUNSHINE" did you experience today?

_____

_____

_____

_____

_____

_____

_____

_____

_____

_____

_____

_____

_____

_____

_____

_____

_____

_____

_____

_____

_____

Sunshine Loves You!

Write It Out & Meditate...

1st Peter 5:4

_____

_____

_____

_____

_____

Talk to God...

_____

_____

_____

_____

_____

_____

_____

_____

_____

_____

_____

_____

God loves you MORE!

What "SUNSHINE" did you experience today?

_____
_____
_____
_____
_____
_____
_____
_____
_____
_____
_____
_____
_____
_____
_____
_____
_____
_____
_____
_____
_____
_____

Sunshine Loves You!

Write It Out & Meditate...

Philippians 4:4

_____
_____
_____
_____
_____

Talk to God...

_____
_____
_____
_____
_____
_____
_____
_____
_____
_____
_____

God loves you MORE!

What "SUNSHINE" did you experience today?

_____

_____

_____

_____

_____

_____

_____

_____

_____

_____

_____

_____

_____

_____

_____

_____

_____

_____

_____

_____

_____

Sunshine Loves You!

Write It Out & Meditate...

Proverbs 17:22

_____

_____

_____

_____

_____

Talk to God...

_____

_____

_____

_____

_____

_____

_____

_____

_____

_____

_____

God loves you MORE!

What "SUNSHINE" did you experience today?

_____

_____

_____

_____

_____

_____

_____

_____

_____

_____

_____

_____

_____

_____

_____

_____

_____

_____

_____

_____

_____

Sunshine Loves You!

Write It Out & Meditate...

2nd Corinthians 1:3-4

_____

_____

_____

_____

_____

Talk to God...

_____

_____

_____

_____

_____

_____

_____

_____

_____

_____

_____

God loves you MORE!

What "SUNSHINE" did you experience today?

_____

_____

_____

_____

_____

_____

_____

_____

_____

_____

_____

_____

_____

_____

_____

_____

_____

_____

_____

_____

Sunshine Loves You!

Write It Out & Meditate...

Psalm 91:11-12

_____

_____

_____

_____

_____

Talk to God...

_____

_____

_____

_____

_____

_____

_____

_____

_____

_____

_____

_____

God loves you MORE!

What "SUNSHINE" did you experience today?

_____

_____

_____

_____

_____

_____

_____

_____

_____

_____

_____

_____

_____

_____

_____

_____

_____

_____

_____

_____

_____

Sunshine Loves You!

Write It Out & Meditate...

1st Thessalonians 5:16

_____
_____
_____
_____
_____

Talk to God...

_____
_____
_____
_____
_____
_____
_____
_____
_____
_____
_____

God loves you MORE!

What "SUNSHINE" did you experience today?

_____

_____

_____

_____

_____

_____

_____

_____

_____

_____

_____

_____

_____

_____

_____

_____

_____

_____

_____

_____

Sunshine Loves You!

November 23, 2021

Write It Out & Meditate...

Psalm 118:24

_____

_____

_____

_____

_____

Talk to God...

_____

_____

_____

_____

_____

_____

_____

_____

_____

_____

_____

_____

God loves you MORE!

What "SUNSHINE" did you experience today?

_____
_____
_____
_____
_____
_____
_____
_____
_____
_____
_____
_____
_____
_____
_____
_____
_____
_____
_____
_____
_____

Sunshine Loves You!

Write It Out & Meditate...

Romans 12:13

_____

_____

_____

_____

_____

Talk to God...

_____

_____

_____

_____

_____

_____

_____

_____

_____

_____

_____

God loves you MORE!

What "SUNSHINE" did you experience today?

_____

_____

_____

_____

_____

_____

_____

_____

_____

_____

_____

_____

_____

_____

_____

_____

_____

_____

_____

_____

Sunshine Loves You!

Write It Out & Meditate...

1st Thessalonians 5:22

_____
_____
_____
_____
_____

Talk to God...

_____
_____
_____
_____
_____
_____
_____
_____
_____
_____
_____
_____

God loves you MORE!

What "SUNSHINE" did you experience today?

_____

_____

_____

_____

_____

_____

_____

_____

_____

_____

_____

_____

_____

_____

_____

_____

_____

_____

_____

_____

Sunshine Loves You!

Write It Out & Meditate...

1st Samuel 2:9

_____

_____

_____

_____

_____

Talk to God...

_____

_____

_____

_____

_____

_____

_____

_____

_____

_____

_____

God loves you MORE!

What "SUNSHINE" did you experience today?

_____

_____

_____

_____

_____

_____

_____

_____

_____

_____

_____

_____

_____

_____

_____

_____

_____

_____

_____

_____

_____

Sunshine Loves You!

November 27, 2021

Write It Out & Meditate...

1st Corinthians 13:4-5

_____
_____
_____
_____
_____

Talk to God...

_____
_____
_____
_____
_____
_____
_____
_____
_____
_____
_____

God loves you MORE!

What "SUNSHINE" did you experience today?

_____

_____

_____

_____

_____

_____

_____

_____

_____

_____

_____

_____

_____

_____

_____

_____

_____

_____

Sunshine Loves You!

Write It Out & Meditate...

Matthew 5:13

_____

_____

_____

_____

_____

Talk to God...

_____

_____

_____

_____

_____

_____

_____

_____

_____

_____

_____

God loves you MORE!

What "SUNSHINE" did you experience today?

_____

_____

_____

_____

_____

_____

_____

_____

_____

_____

_____

_____

_____

_____

_____

_____

Sunshine Loves You!

Write It Out & Meditate...

Romans 12:17

_____
_____
_____
_____
_____

Talk to God...

_____
_____
_____
_____
_____
_____
_____
_____
_____
_____
_____

God loves you MORE!

What "SUNSHINE" did you experience today?

_____

_____

_____

_____

_____

_____

_____

_____

_____

_____

_____

_____

_____

_____

_____

_____

_____

_____

Sunshine Loves You!

Write It Out & Meditate...

1st John 4:16

_____
_____
_____
_____
_____

Talk to God...

_____
_____
_____
_____
_____
_____
_____
_____
_____
_____
_____

God loves you MORE!

What "SUNSHINE" did you experience today?

_____

_____

_____

_____

_____

_____

_____

_____

_____

_____

_____

_____

_____

_____

_____

_____

_____

_____

_____

Sunshine Loves You!

December's
Scripture Focus

"I am leaving you with a

gift-peace of mind and heart.

And the peace I give is a gift the

world cannot give.

So don't be troubled or afraid."

John 14:27 NLT

My thoughts about this Scripture:

_____

_____

_____

_____

_____

God loves you MORE!

Sunshine Loves You!

December's Reflection & Prayer

This is a GREAT MONTH to develop kindness and operate in one of God's greatest treasures: being a peacemaker. Allow God to use you to help kindle the embers when you sense dissension arising between you and someone or between others. God left you with the peace of mind and heart. Someone else doesn't know that they have been given this gift. Give the gift of peace away to someone by being a walking peacemaker. Offer an apology, though you weren't wrong. Offer a genuine smile to the individual who mean mugs you. Offer to pay for an adversary's lunch. Someone will test you, but you are equipped to win the battle because you are choosing to take the high road, knowing that this unique gift was given to you and you want to honor the One who gave it to you.

Father, I thank you for giving good gifts: gifts like your son Jesus and the gift of peace. When my world begins to feel like a tornado is happening, with things feeling out of place and out of control, help me to remain stable in my mind, knowing that you have left me with the gift of peace of mind and heart. Continue to work on me God and help me to learn how to remain calm in all situations. I understand that both my physical and mental health are affected when I allow people, places and things to affect me. Help me to be like the ship on the waves during a storm, knowing that you have it all under control.

In Jesus' Name,

AMEN.

God loves you MORE!

December 2021 (United States)

January 2022

S	M	T	W	T	F	S
						1
2	3	4	5	6	7	8
9	10	11	12	13	14	15
16	17	18	19	20	21	22
23	24	25	26	27	28	29
30	31					

Sun	Mon	Tue	Wed	Thu	Fri	Sat
28	29	30	1	2	3	4 ● New Moon
5	6	7	8	9	10 ◐ 1st Quarter	11
12	13	14	15	16	17	18 ○ Full Moon
19	20	21	22	23	24 ● 'Christmas Day' day off Christmas Eve	25 Christmas Day
26 ◑ 3rd Quarter	27	28	29	30	31 ● 'New Year's Day' day off New Year's Eve	1 New Year's Day

● Federal Holidays   ● Local Holidays   ●) Multiple Events

Sunshine Loves You!

December 1, 2021

Write It Out & Meditate...

2nd Corinthians 9:8

_____
_____
_____
_____
_____

Talk to God...

_____
_____
_____
_____
_____
_____
_____
_____
_____
_____
_____

God loves you MORE!

What "SUNSHINE" did you experience today?

_____

_____

_____

_____

_____

_____

_____

_____

_____

_____

_____

_____

_____

_____

_____

_____

_____

_____

_____

Sunshine Loves You!

Write It Out & Meditate...

1st Corinthians 13:6-7

_____

_____

_____

_____

_____

Talk to God...

_____

_____

_____

_____

_____

_____

_____

_____

_____

_____

_____

God loves you MORE!

What "SUNSHINE" did you experience today?

_____

_____

_____

_____

_____

_____

_____

_____

_____

_____

_____

_____

_____

_____

_____

_____

_____

_____

_____

Sunshine Loves You!

December 3, 2021

Write It Out & Meditate...

1ˢᵗ John 3:1

_____
_____
_____
_____
_____

Talk to God...

_____
_____
_____
_____
_____
_____
_____
_____
_____
_____
_____

God loves you MORE!

What "SUNSHINE" did you experience today?

_____

_____

_____

_____

_____

_____

_____

_____

_____

_____

_____

_____

_____

_____

_____

_____

_____

_____

_____

_____

Sunshine Loves You!

Write It Out & Meditate...

Jeremiah 33:8

_____

_____

_____

_____

_____

Talk to God...

_____

_____

_____

_____

_____

_____

_____

_____

_____

_____

_____

_____

God loves you MORE!

What "SUNSHINE" did you experience today?

_____

_____

_____

_____

_____

_____

_____

_____

_____

_____

_____

_____

_____

_____

_____

_____

_____

_____

_____

_____

Sunshine Loves You!

Write It Out & Meditate...

1st Thessalonians 5:17

_____
_____
_____
_____
_____

Talk to God...

_____
_____
_____
_____
_____
_____
_____
_____
_____
_____
_____

God loves you MORE!

What "SUNSHINE" did you experience today?

_____

_____

_____

_____

_____

_____

_____

_____

_____

_____

_____

_____

_____

_____

_____

_____

_____

_____

_____

_____

_____

Sunshine Loves You!

Write It Out & Meditate...

1st Samuel 16:7

_____
_____
_____
_____
_____

Talk to God...

_____
_____
_____
_____
_____
_____
_____
_____
_____
_____
_____

God loves you MORE!

What "SUNSHINE" did you experience today?

_____

_____

_____

_____

_____

_____

_____

_____

_____

_____

_____

_____

_____

_____

_____

_____

_____

_____

_____

_____

Sunshine Loves You!

Write It Out & Meditate...

Psalm 30:5

_____

_____

_____

_____

_____

Talk to God...

_____

_____

_____

_____

_____

_____

_____

_____

_____

_____

_____

_____

God loves you MORE!

What "SUNSHINE" did you experience today?

_____

_____

_____

_____

_____

_____

_____

_____

_____

_____

_____

_____

_____

_____

_____

_____

_____

_____

_____

_____

Sunshine Loves You!

Write It Out & Meditate...

1st Corinthians 16:14

_____
_____
_____
_____
_____

Talk to God...

_____
_____
_____
_____
_____
_____
_____
_____
_____
_____
_____

God loves you MORE!

What "SUNSHINE" did you experience today?

_____

_____

_____

_____

_____

_____

_____

_____

_____

_____

_____

_____

_____

_____

_____

_____

_____

_____

_____

_____

Sunshine Loves You!

Write It Out & Meditate...

Romans 12:14

_____

_____

_____

_____

_____

Talk to God...

_____

_____

_____

_____

_____

_____

_____

_____

_____

_____

_____

God loves you MORE!

What "SUNSHINE" did you experience today?

_____

_____

_____

_____

_____

_____

_____

_____

_____

_____

_____

_____

_____

_____

_____

_____

_____

_____

_____

Sunshine Loves You!

Write It Out & Meditate...

1st Thessalonians 5:18

_____

_____

_____

_____

_____

Talk to God...

_____

_____

_____

_____

_____

_____

_____

_____

_____

_____

_____

_____

God loves you MORE!

What "SUNSHINE" did you experience today?

_____

_____

_____

_____

_____

_____

_____

_____

_____

_____

_____

_____

_____

_____

_____

_____

_____

_____

Sunshine Loves You!

Write It Out & Meditate...

Psalm 89:33

_____
_____
_____
_____
_____

Talk to God...

_____
_____
_____
_____
_____
_____
_____
_____
_____
_____
_____
_____

God loves you MORE!

What "SUNSHINE" did you experience today?

_____

_____

_____

_____

_____

_____

_____

_____

_____

_____

_____

_____

_____

_____

_____

_____

_____

_____

_____

Sunshine Loves You!

December 12, 2021

Write It Out & Meditate...

Matthew 21:22

_____
_____
_____
_____
_____

Talk to God...

_____
_____
_____
_____
_____
_____
_____
_____
_____
_____
_____

God loves you MORE!

What "SUNSHINE" did you experience today?

_____

_____

_____

_____

_____

_____

_____

_____

_____

_____

_____

_____

_____

_____

_____

_____

_____

_____

_____

Sunshine Loves You!

Write It Out & Meditate...

Romans 13:8

_____
_____
_____
_____
_____

Talk to God...

_____
_____
_____
_____
_____
_____
_____
_____
_____
_____
_____
_____

God loves you MORE!

What "SUNSHINE" did you experience today?

_____

_____

_____

_____

_____

_____

_____

_____

_____

_____

_____

_____

_____

_____

_____

_____

_____

_____

_____

Sunshine Loves You!

Write It Out & Meditate...

Psalm 16:11

_____
_____
_____
_____
_____

Talk to God...

_____
_____
_____
_____
_____
_____
_____
_____
_____
_____
_____

God loves you MORE!

What "SUNSHINE" did you experience today?

_____
_____
_____
_____
_____
_____
_____
_____
_____
_____
_____
_____
_____
_____
_____
_____
_____
_____
_____
_____

Sunshine Loves You!

Write It Out & Meditate...

John 15:13

_____
_____
_____
_____
_____

Talk to God...

_____
_____
_____
_____
_____
_____
_____
_____
_____
_____
_____

God loves you MORE!

What "SUNSHINE" did you experience today?

_____

_____

_____

_____

_____

_____

_____

_____

_____

_____

_____

_____

_____

_____

_____

_____

_____

_____

_____

Sunshine Loves You!

December 16, 2021

Write It Out & Meditate...

Romans 12:19

_____
_____
_____
_____
_____

Talk to God...

_____
_____
_____
_____
_____
_____
_____
_____
_____
_____
_____

God loves you MORE!

What "SUNSHINE" did you experience today?

_____

_____

_____

_____

_____

_____

_____

_____

_____

_____

_____

_____

_____

_____

_____

_____

_____

_____

_____

_____

Sunshine Loves You!

Write It Out & Meditate...

Psalm 121:3

_____
_____
_____
_____
_____

Talk to God...

_____
_____
_____
_____
_____
_____
_____
_____
_____
_____
_____

God loves you MORE!

What "SUNSHINE" did you experience today?

_____

_____

_____

_____

_____

_____

_____

_____

_____

_____

_____

_____

_____

_____

_____

_____

_____

_____

_____

_____

_____

Sunshine Loves You!

Write It Out & Meditate...

Mark 12:31

_____

_____

_____

_____

_____

Talk to God...

_____

_____

_____

_____

_____

_____

_____

_____

_____

_____

_____

_____

God loves you MORE!

What "SUNSHINE" did you experience today?

_____

_____

_____

_____

_____

_____

_____

_____

_____

_____

_____

_____

_____

_____

_____

_____

_____

_____

_____

Sunshine Loves You!

Write It Out & Meditate...

Romans 12:16

_____
_____
_____
_____
_____

Talk to God...

_____
_____
_____
_____
_____
_____
_____
_____
_____
_____
_____
_____

God loves you MORE!

What "SUNSHINE" did you experience today?

_____

_____

_____

_____

_____

_____

_____

_____

_____

_____

_____

_____

_____

_____

_____

_____

_____

_____

_____

_____

_____

Sunshine Loves You!

Write It Out & Meditate...

Hebrews 7:25

_____
_____
_____
_____
_____

Talk to God...

_____
_____
_____
_____
_____
_____
_____
_____
_____
_____
_____

God loves you MORE!

What "SUNSHINE" did you experience today?

_____

_____

_____

_____

_____

_____

_____

_____

_____

_____

_____

_____

_____

_____

_____

_____

_____

_____

Sunshine Loves You!

December 21, 2021

Write It Out & Meditate...

Matthew 5:5

_____
_____
_____
_____
_____

Talk to God...

_____
_____
_____
_____
_____
_____
_____
_____
_____
_____
_____

God loves you MORE!

What "SUNSHINE" did you experience today?

_____

_____

_____

_____

_____

_____

_____

_____

_____

_____

_____

_____

_____

_____

_____

_____

_____

_____

_____

_____

Sunshine Loves You!

December 22, 2021

Write It Out & Meditate...

2ⁿᵈ Timothy 2:13

_____
_____
_____
_____
_____

Talk to God...

_____
_____
_____
_____
_____
_____
_____
_____
_____
_____
_____
_____

God loves you MORE!

What "SUNSHINE" did you experience today?

_____

_____

_____

_____

_____

_____

_____

_____

_____

_____

_____

_____

_____

_____

_____

_____

_____

_____

_____

Sunshine Loves You!

Write It Out & Meditate...

Romans 12:20

_____
_____
_____
_____
_____

Talk to God...

_____
_____
_____
_____
_____
_____
_____
_____
_____
_____

God loves you MORE!

What "SUNSHINE" did you experience today?

_____

_____

_____

_____

_____

_____

_____

_____

_____

_____

_____

_____

_____

_____

_____

_____

_____

_____

_____

_____

_____

Sunshine Loves You!

Write It Out & Meditate...

Proverbs 17:17

_____

_____

_____

_____

_____

Talk to God...

_____

_____

_____

_____

_____

_____

_____

_____

_____

_____

_____

God loves you MORE!

What "SUNSHINE" did you experience today?

_____

_____

_____

_____

_____

_____

_____

_____

_____

_____

_____

_____

_____

_____

_____

_____

_____

_____

_____

_____

Sunshine Loves You!

Write It Out & Meditate...

Isaiah 9:6

_____

_____

_____

_____

_____

Talk to God...

_____

_____

_____

_____

_____

_____

_____

_____

_____

_____

_____

_____

God loves you MORE!

What "SUNSHINE" did you experience today?

_____

_____

_____

_____

_____

_____

_____

_____

_____

_____

_____

_____

_____

_____

_____

_____

_____

_____

_____

Sunshine Loves You!

Write It Out & Meditate...

Psalm 121:7-8

_____

_____

_____

_____

_____

Talk to God...

_____

_____

_____

_____

_____

_____

_____

_____

_____

_____

_____

God loves you MORE!

What "SUNSHINE" did you experience today?

_____

_____

_____

_____

_____

_____

_____

_____

_____

_____

_____

_____

_____

_____

_____

_____

_____

_____

_____

_____

Sunshine Loves You!

December 27, 2021

Write It Out & Meditate...

Romans 5:8

_____
_____
_____
_____
_____

Talk to God...

_____
_____
_____
_____
_____
_____
_____
_____
_____
_____
_____

God loves you MORE!

What "SUNSHINE" did you experience today?

_____

_____

_____

_____

_____

_____

_____

_____

_____

_____

_____

_____

_____

_____

_____

_____

_____

_____

_____

Sunshine Loves You!

Write It Out & Meditate...

Colossians 3:15

_____

_____

_____

_____

_____

Talk to God...

_____

_____

_____

_____

_____

_____

_____

_____

_____

_____

_____

God loves you MORE!

What "SUNSHINE" did you experience today?

_____

_____

_____

_____

_____

_____

_____

_____

_____

_____

_____

_____

_____

_____

_____

_____

_____

_____

_____

_____

Sunshine Loves You!

December 29, 2021

Write It Out & Meditate...

Romans 12:18

_____
_____
_____
_____
_____

Talk to God...

_____
_____
_____
_____
_____
_____
_____
_____
_____
_____
_____

God loves you MORE!

What "SUNSHINE" did you experience today?

_____

_____

_____

_____

_____

_____

_____

_____

_____

_____

_____

_____

_____

_____

_____

_____

_____

_____

_____

Sunshine Loves You!

Write It Out & Meditate...

1st Corinthians 16:3

_____
_____
_____
_____
_____

Talk to God...

_____
_____
_____
_____
_____
_____
_____
_____
_____
_____
_____

God loves you MORE!

What "SUNSHINE" did you experience today?

_____

_____

_____

_____

_____

_____

_____

_____

_____

_____

_____

_____

_____

_____

_____

_____

_____

_____

_____

Sunshine Loves You!

Write It Out & Meditate...

Isaiah 43:18-19

_____

_____

_____

_____

_____

Talk to God...

_____

_____

_____

_____

_____

_____

_____

_____

_____

_____

_____

God loves you MORE!

What "SUNSHINE" did you experience today?

_____

_____
_____
_____
_____
_____
_____
_____
_____
_____
_____
_____
_____
_____
_____
_____
_____
_____
_____
_____
_____

Sunshine Loves You!

CPSIA information can be obtained
at www.ICGtesting.com
Printed in the USA
LVHW080533120321
681280LV00003B/4